SWORDFISH
AT WAR

SWORDFISH
AT WAR

Previous page:
**This picture aboard *Tracker*
shows to good effect the
cramped conditions below
decks as this Swordfish is
brought up for another anti-
submarine sweep.**
IWM (A19705)

Below:
**Not the way to arrive on
deck landing training
flights — but it's a lovely
picture of a Swordfish,
though, showing off the
camouflage pattern. Note
that both wingtips are
crumpled.** *R. Fitzsimmonds*

W. HARRISON

SWORDFISH AT WAR

LONDON

IAN ALLAN LTD

Acknowledgements

There can be little doubt that without the valuable assistance of the many people who were involved with the Swordfish, the writing of this book would have been so much more difficult, if not impossible. What one has to appreciate is that in allowing me into their homes, logbooks, diaries, scrapbooks, photo albums and, often, the most intimate of memories that become a part of our island's history — that they were there, they made it! I hope future generations take note of the spirit that prevailed in those times of adversity — and are proud of it.

Acknowledgements there must be, the first going to my wife and family who believed in me. Particular thanks to John Powner and his staff for their unstinting help with photographic problems; to Eric 'Ginger' Tyler for his exciting contributions; and to all the following who have contributed so much: J. Adams, G. Aitken, E. Bond and J. Bryant of the Telegraphist Air Gunners Association; J. T. Canham; J. K. Cannon; A. D. Corkhill; Canon R. G. Chaffey-Moore; Cdr C. R. Coxon MVO, RN (Retd); G. T. A. Darley; A. Emmerson; Cdr R. N. Everett OBE, RN (Retd); R. Fitzsimmonds; T. Fagg, F. Grainger; 'Nat' Gold; S. Gurton of the RAFA; D. Hall; A. Hodgins; Lt-Cdr M. B. W. Howell; C. R. Jeffs, F. V. Jones; L. J. Kelly DSC; Lt-Cdr R. E. F. Kerrison; H. Liddle; E. B. Mackenzie; Cdr N. Martin RN (Retd); J. S. G. Mitchell, C. E. Orvis, T. Mogford; J. J. Pinkerton; Lt-Cdr F. C. Rice DSM, RN (Retd); A. Rudd; W. H. Scott; Capt T. Shaw DSC, RN (Retd); A. B. Singleton; R. A. Stamp; Cdr J. H. Stenning RN (Retd); Cdr S. H. Suthers DSC, RN (Retd); W. Sleigh; J. K. G. Taylor; J. O. R. Tupper; Capt L. E. D. Walthall DSC, RN (Retd); Lt-Cdr E. W. Whitley; Capt K. Williamson DSO, RN (Retd); Lt-Cdr C. Wines DCM, RN (Retd); A. N. Angus; L. H. T. Ashburner, Mary Ellis, H. Leach, Mrs Pam Henson, C. Tutt and F. Zollner of the Air Transport Auxiliary Association; T. Heffernan of the A&AEE Boscombe Down; M. Willis and A. Williams of the Photographic Department, Imperial War Museum; Capt F. M. A. Torrens-Spence DSO, DSC, AFC; Lord Kilbracken (previously Lt-Cdr J. Godley DSC, RNVR) for allowing me to quote from *Bring back my Stringbag*; Blandford Books Co for permission to use 'Empty Stringbag on the Safi strip' from *Echoes in the Sky*, edited by Ronald Nixon. *Bill Harrison*

Below:
Swordfish NF410 'NH-F' of 119 Squadron which, as part of No 155 GR Wing, operated from Manston and Belgium in support of RAF Coastal Command during 1944/45. Many of the aircraft had cartoon characters painted on; this one has Donald Duck just above the ASV radome. *IWM (CL2286)*

First published 1987

ISBN 0 7110 1676 3

Published by Ian Allan Ltd, Shepperton, Surrey; and printed by Ian Allan Printing Ltd at their works at Coombelands in Runnymede, England

Prints of photographs credited to the Imperial War Museum are for sale on application to its Department of Photographs, Lambeth Road, London SE1 6HZ.

CONTENTS

CONTENTS

Below:

A pleasing study of Merchant Navy Swordfish LS219 'E3' from the Amastra. *J. K. G. Taylor*

INTRODUCTION

'All Swordfish are downgraded to training' — so said an Admiralty signal of 24 July 1945 which brought to an end the operational career of arguably the most famous biplane of all time, and the end of an era.

Between 1939 and 1945, Swordfish were responsible for sinking over 350,000 tons of enemy shipping, took part in the destruction of more than 12 U-boats, and sank or caused serious damage to approximately 30 major enemy ships. However, readers will find that the pages of this book are not just of events on mine-laying, bombing, torpedo and rocket projectile attacks, because *Swordfish at War* is the story of a lady taken to war by young men who flew her, flew in her and worked on her, whether operating from shore stations or aircraft carriers. Stories are legion of when she was flown in every weather imaginable — often when as they say, even the birds weren't flying — and of returning from a mission to land back on a flight deck moving up and down through over 60ft, and slewing sideways as well; of frozen crews having to be lifted from open cockpits after flying in Arctic conditions; all this, and more, in a biplane which rarely exceeded 90kt in level flight. Despite this, she enamoured herself to all who came into contact with her — and some who didn't.

This book, then, is not just of the Swordfish but of those who helped to make her the legend she is. To me there can be no substitute for first-hand accounts and much of the book has been put together from contributions by those who were involved at the time. To most of them the events they talk about are as vivid today as when they happened — and if coloured a little by the years, so be it, they were there. I salute them and delight in using as many of their stories as possible — beginning with this small item by ex-observer David Corkhill:

'I left 819 Squadron on 10 October 1943 to take the Air Signal Officer's course at Arbroath. Stan Brilliant flew me up from Inskip in Swordfish HS293 with my luggage after a farewell lunch. The lunch had the inevitable effects on our bladders for which the Swordfish was not equipped. Stan picked a large and remote field and we landed, achieved blissful relief and took off again. I shudder to think what this would have been reported as in today's newspapers!'

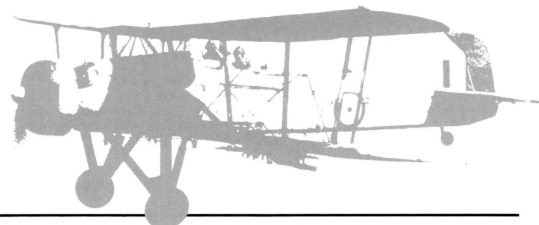

THE BEGINNING OF A LEGEND

Below:
The Fairey PV TSR, powered by an Armstrong Siddeley Panther engine and already bearing a resemblance to a Swordfish, is seen here at Fairey's Great West Aerodrome, now absorbed into London Heathrow airport.

The final design that became the Swordfish was actually something of a hybrid: the Fairey company had carried out design studies for a two-seat torpedo bomber to Specification M1/30, then it prepared designs for a fleet spotter/reconnaissance aircraft to Specification S9/30, and to cap it all it was at that time working on a replacement design for the Greek Naval Air Arm Fairey IIIF Mk IIIB aircraft then in use. The resemblance between the requirements for the three aircraft was such that Fairey put all its eggs in one basket (although the Greeks soon lost interest) and came up with one design to satisfy both requirements for the Air Ministry (which was then still responsible for all naval air matters — to the consternation of the Admiralty). The design team at Fairey was headed at that time by a domiciled Belgian named Marcel Lobelle and in January 1933 they submitted their plans to the Air Ministry for a Fairey PV (Private Venture) Ship-plane (TSR). The original requirements had been for a machine with a 46ft wing span, reducing to 18ft when folded, 37ft in length, and 14ft 9in in height. The maximum speed at 8,000ft was to be

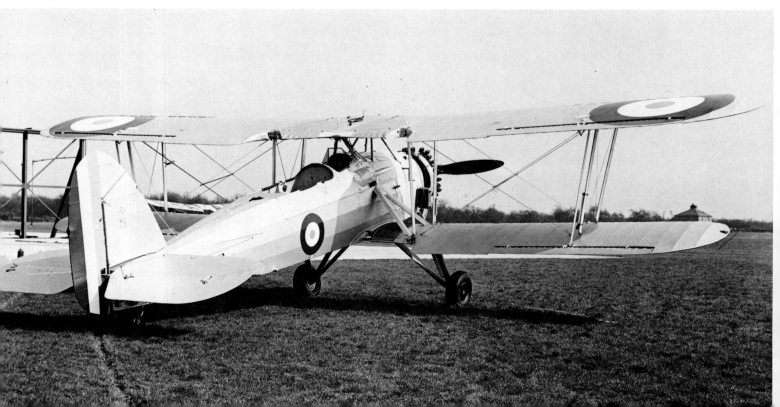

140kt and it was to have a landing speed of 50kt. The fixed armament was to be one machine gun mounted in the forward fuselage, with 600 rounds of ammunition. The design also had to allow conversion from land to floatplane without any problems, and the structure had to be stressed to withstand catapulting from carrier decks or cruiser catapults, and also to take arresting loads on landing. Power plant initially was a moderately supercharged Rolls-Royce Kestrel engine but the design had to allow easy conversion to alternative air- or water-cooled aero engines. Meanwhile, the Air Ministry was considering the submitted plans, and changes were already in the pipeline from the Technical Office at Fairey. Most notable was the change to air-cooled power in the form of a moderately supercharged Armstrong Siddeley 625hp Panther VI engine. (Later still, this was changed to the Bristol Pegasus.)

To everyone's delight, Fairey received the go-ahead to build a prototype; it was flown for the first time on 21 March 1933 from the aerodrome at Harmondsworth, which wasn't far from the present London Heathrow Airport. The pilot was one of the most well known of prewar British test pilots, the dashing Flt Lt Chris Staniland, who was an ace motorcycle and racing car driver, an ex-RAF fighter pilot and Fairey's chief test and display pilot. With the success of the first flight the Air Ministry informed Fairey that it was issuing a new Specification, S15/33, which was to cover the construction of the service general purpose aircraft intended for

Top:
Flt Lt Chris Staniland running up the re-engined PV TSR prior to a test flight. It was while spinning this machine from 14,000ft that he got into difficulties and had to bale out — but got flung in to the rear cockpit.

Above:
The prototype Swordfish K4190, before it had been silver doped, being run up. The excellent facilities at the Great West Aerodrome can partly be seen in the background.

Left:
The newly sprayed prototype K4190 with two-blade propeller.

9

the Fleet Air Arm. The only change specified was that the gross weight for flying was not to exceed 7,500lb, as ships' catapults were not capable of launching aircraft with an all-up weight over 8,000lb.

After some preliminary flying trials the Panther VI was changed to a Bristol Pegasus IIM radial engine driving a Watts two-blade wooden propeller, and Flt Lt Staniland flew the machine in its revised form on 10 July 1933. The aircraft also had spats on the wheels, and a later mod included an arrester hook for anticipated service trials. Test flying continued apace until 11 September 1933, when Staniland had one of the most interesting and hair-raising escapades in the annals of flying. On that day he was conducting spinning trials at different loadings but was having difficulty in introducing the aircraft to spin. On one flight (the last!) he initiated a right-hand spin from 14,000ft which, without any warning, suddenly became very flat with fast rotation and the nose well up. Normal recovery actions only caused the aircraft to shake violently and after about 12 turns he decided to abandon the recovery and bale out. As the spin was to the right he elected to leave to the left and thus avoid getting caught up on

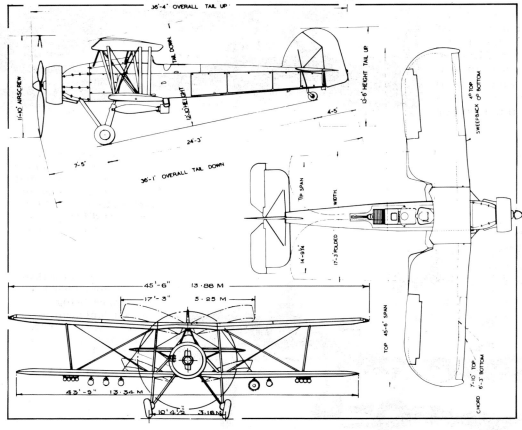

Top:
Staines reservoir is seen coming up under the nose of the prototype as Flt Lt Staniland starts to put it through its paces.
Flight International

Above:
K4190 after being converted into a dual control machine, now with a three-blade propeller. It was later converted back into a standard aircraft and put into use at Gosport.

Left:
The Fairey Aviation Co Swordfish landplane, general arrangement, from a company drawing.

Top right:
This air-to-air view of K5933 shows off to good effect the layout of the machine.
Real Photographs

Right:
The Fairey Swordfish seaplane, general arrangement, from a company drawing.

anything. However, due to the slip-stream and gravity forces he was flung into the rear cockpit! Somewhat perturbed he managed to extricate himself and finally succeeded in getting out before the aircraft crashed at Longford in Middlesex.

On 25 and 26 September, all the departments involved with the aircraft, such as the drawing office, flight test department, technical office, etc, suggested that although changes were required, the policy should be one of modification rather than any radical redesign. From experience gained any modifications would hopefully lead to a simpler, easy to maintain aircraft. As an example, the experimental department alone asked for 78 minor changes to be incorporated in any second machine. Much discussion was made about the flat spin problem and Staniland himself suggested some changes including using a three-blade metal propeller instead of the wooden one. In the early test flights Staniland said that he had experienced tail buffeting at low speeds with some fore and aft instability.

A decision was made to construct another machine incorporating many of the changes; to differentiate it from the earlier aircraft it would be known as the TSR II, with the Air Ministry allotting

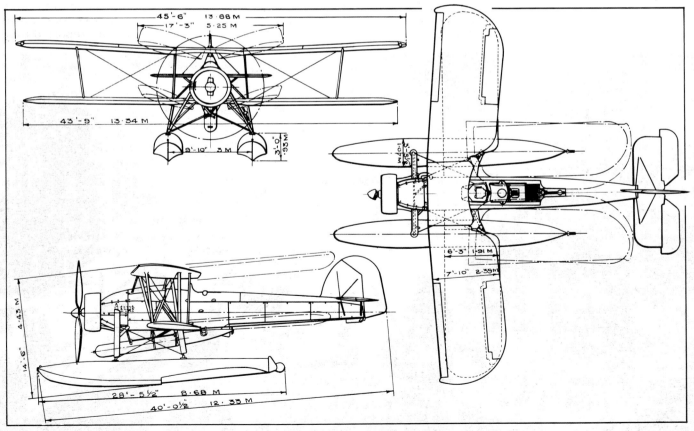

the serial K4190 for service trials. Although externally similar to the previous aircraft it had a longer fuselage (an extra bay being added), and to compensate for this, a 4° sweepback on the upper wings was incorporated. The engine was changed to a Pegasus IIIM3 with a wide chord Townend ring fixed at seven points. More noticeable were the anti-spin strakes on the rear fuselage just forward of the tailplane. The fin and rudder were of greater chord than before but construction in general was similar to the first aircraft.

Chris Staniland took K4190 into the air for the first time on 17 April 1934 from Fairey's own airfield, the Great West Aerodrome, now incorporated into London Heathrow Airport. After the two months of contractor's trials some 91 further improvements were added, many of a very small nature, then K4190 left for further trials at Martlesham Heath in June 1934. (Before World War 2 all civil and military aircraft were tested at the Aeroplane & Armament Experimental Establishment which was based at Martlesham Heath.) Although the trials report was favourable toward the TSR II, there was some criticism about slow recovery from spins, stalling and, when loaded to an aft C of G, fore and aft instability. Controls were reported to be

light and effective but the ailerons were prone to snatch at the stall or in spins. With the slots open at the stall there was a tendency to roll. Spins were carried out with weights up to 7,500lb to represent a torpedo load, but in dives up to 210kt and with aft loading, the aircraft still suffered from longitudinal instability. Eventually a cure was found by changing the elevator movement ranges.

The aircraft then went to the Royal Aircraft Establishment at Farnborough for catapult trials and then moved on to the aircraft carrier HMS *Courageous* for deck landing trials. During November, K4190 returned to the Fairey factory at Hamble where Staniland flew it on twin floats and later conducted floatplane catapult trials from the battlecruiser HMS *Repulse*. Next stop was the Marine Aircraft Experimental Establishment at Felixstowe where it was examined from the maintenance and repair point of view. After a favourable report the aircraft moved to the Torpedo Trials Unit at Gosport, where it crashed on a hedge between the barrack blocks in February 1935.

The aircraft was then subjected to a complete rebuild before emerging again in January 1936. It was used by Fairey for a short time to test various improvements such as modified ailerons, oleo legs, dual controls, a larger diameter tailwheel, etc, until 6 September 1937,

Top:
Wings being assembled in the Blackburn factory.
British Aerospace

Above:
The beginning of the final assembly line. As components come in from the sub-contractors the structure begins to take shape.

Right:
The final assembly line at Sherburn-in-Elmet, Yorkshire. Much of the production flying was done by Flt Lt H. P. Wilson. He had joined the RAF in 1926 and after a spell instructing in civil aero clubs rejoined the RAF to instruct, but was later seconded to Blackburn for production test flying.
British Aerospace

when K4190 was taken on charge by the Fleet Air Arm at Gosport.

Earlier, with the success of K4190, the Air Ministry issued Specification S38/34 calling for three further development aircraft, K5660, K5661 and K5662, to be built from the modified drawings of K4190, and decreed that henceforth the machines would be known as Swordfish. With the order for three preproduction aircraft came another for 86 Mk 1 Swordfish, and this was quickly followed by another order for 131.

Initial production was centred at the Fairey factory at Hayes, where one was turned out in 1935, 147 in 1936, 201 in 1937, 143 in 1938, 197 in 1939 and three in 1940; production was then transferred to Blackburn at Brough. The first Blackburn-built Swordfish, V4288, was test flown by Fairey's pilot, Flt Lt F. H. Dixon, on 1 December 1940; thereafter Blackburn produced 415 in 1941, 271 in 1942, 592 in 1943 and 420 in 1944, when production ceased with NS204. Thus Fairey produced 692 aircraft and Blackburn 1,699. Swordfish production had been transferred to Blackburn's because Fairey had other production commitments such as the Albacore, Barracuda and Firefly — it was Capt M. S. (later Rear-Adm Sir Matthew) Slattery, the Admiralty Director of Air Materiel, who suggested that

Blackburn could take on the extra work. By the end of 1940 the new assembly plant had been set up at Sherburn-in-Elmet, between Leeds and Selby. Under the dispersal arrangement to reduce the risk of bombing of factories and to spread the workload, many small firms in the Leeds area produced parts for the Swordfish, such as Appleyard which made wings, Tate's which made centre sections and Thomas Green which produced the stubplanes and undercarriage.

Unofficially the Swordfish produced by Blackburn were known as Blackfish, and the author has even seen such entries in logbooks; interestingly, experienced pilots claimed that they could tell the difference when flying a Fairey or Blackburn machine. Another one for the squadron line book no doubt!

The basic Swordfish remained the same throughout its production life. The only other versions were the Mk II, which had strengthened lower wings to take metal skin undersurfaces so as to launch rocket projectiles without damaging the wing; and the Mk III, which, apart from the same mod as the Mk II on its lower wings, had built-in air-to-surface (ASV) radar in a radome between the undercarriage legs. Some Mk IIs sent to Canada were modified to have enclosed cockpits, and were known locally as Swordfish Mk IVs.

Above:
An excellent shot of an early production Swordfish from the Hayes factory showing the wing-folding arrangement. The storage space in carrier- or shore-based hangars was always put to better use with Swordfish parked like this.

14

EVERY PICTURE TELLS A STORY...

Below:
Swordfish K8396 hangs precariously over the side of *Eagle* after the incident mentioned in the text.
E. B. Mackenzie

Below right:
Released, the Swordfish settles in the water, a total loss. *E. B. Mackenzie*

In February 1937, the carrier HMS *Eagle* embarked nine Swordfish of 813 Squadron and sailed for the China station, where she relieved *Hermes* and took over the Fairey Seals of 824 Squadron at the same time. By mid-1938 the Seals had been replaced by Swordfish so that the ship had 18 for spotting, general reconnaissance and, if necessary, strike duties. The duties were, in the main, to protect British interests in the area.

During April 1939 a new young Telegraphist Air Gunner, E. W. F. 'Ginger' Tyler, joined 813 Squadron, and he quickly settled into the life of carrier flying. He had not been with the squadron long before he had an experience that he has remembered to the present day. He recalls:

'I was the regular TAG flying in Swordfish K8396 from *Eagle*. A few days before 6 June 1939 a newly qualified pilot joined 813 Squadron when we were at Wei-Hai-Wei; his name was Lt Parker. The fleet went to sea on 6 June and as flying exercises were being carried out it provided an opportunity for Lt Parker to complete his training in deck landing on the *Eagle*.

'We took off at about 09.00hrs for local flying and dive-bombing practice which should have been followed by three deck landings. No observer was necessary so a volunteer who had asked for a flight was carried. I don't remember the man's name but he was a stoker about 30 years of age. The local flying being completed, we approached the ship for the first deck landing. Everything appeared to be going well until the last minute, when the pilot appeared to be a little worried about getting too near the island, and veered over to the port side of the ship. He just managed to pick up the last arrester wire before the port wheel went over into the nets, and the Swordfish slowly turned upside down, being held only by one wheel lodged in the nets. We, the crew, were left hanging upside down held only by the safety wires (we called them G-strings). I did notice that there was a lot of petrol vapour around the engine, which did not help.

'The flight deck crew immediately went into action and ropes were thrown over the skyward-looking belly of the aircraft for the crew to clamber down into the sea. The first man down was the stoker, who was screaming his head off. I told him to grab the rope and lower himself into the sea. He screamed that he couldn't swim. At this I slipped his G-string and down he went, to be picked up out of the water by the ship's whaler. Next one down was the pilot, Lt Parker, who was lowered, none too gently, into the sea, and got a good dunking by the flight deck party before being retrieved by the whaler. I was the last one down and waited until the whaler was almost underneath me before descending, and therefore escaped a ducking.

'There was no way the aircraft could be salvaged so the holding tyre was punctured and the Swordfish dropped into the sea. The next day the same pilot took another Swordfish up and did exactly the same thing! Fortunately I wasn't with him that time, but he was immediately posted to a cruiser — and not for flying duties either!'

Below:
Lt H. Parker's second Swordfish about to be released to the sea.
E. B. Mackenzie
Bottom:
Total loss No 2 — note the dinghy and the panel from where it was released when the aircraft touched the water. *E. B. Mackenzie*

INTO ACTION — NORWAY 1940

The Norwegian campaign in World War 2, although an embarrassing defeat for the British Government, gave the Fleet Air Arm its first real series of actions against the enemy and proved the strategy of using carrier-borne aircraft. In doing so, it also provided a wealth of operational experience and knowledge which was to prove invaluable as the war progressed.

Germany invaded Norway on 9 April 1940, having already infringed its neutrality by taking iron ore shipments through Norwegian waters. An Allied plan to prevent further such incursions by putting occupation troops ashore was thwarted by the invasion, which rapidly captured ports from Narvik in the north to Bergen some 500 miles to the south.

The British Home Fleet was quickly ordered to Norway to contain and harass the enemy. *Furious*, the only carrier in home waters, was refitting in the Clyde but cut this short and on the 9th embarked her two Swordfish Squadrons, 816 and 818, with a total of 18 aircraft. She sailed on 10 April to join the Home Fleet sailing off Norway — the same day that 25 Skua aircraft of 800 and 803 Squadrons, operating out of Hatston in the Orkneys, carried out a brilliant dive-bombing attack on the German cruiser *Konigsberg* and sank her. On the morning of 11 April *Furious* launched what was to be the first co-ordinated torpedo strike in the history of naval warfare. The German heavy cruiser *Hipper* and four destroyers were believed to be in Trondheim harbour and a strike was laid on. Unbeknown to *Furious*, the *Hipper* and one of its destroyers had already left Trondheim and there were only three enemy destroyers remaining. At first light, Lt-Cdr H. Gardiner leading 816 Squadron and Lt-Cdr J. Fenton leading 818 Squadron took-off to carry out their attack. The local situation required a change of plan and an attack was made against a destroyer at a different anchorage, but the torpedoes failed to hit their target due to shallow water; all the Swordfish returned safely.

The next day *Furious* flew off Swordfish of 818 Squadron at 16.15hrs to attack enemy ships at Narvik. The weather was terrible, with sleet and snowstorms in winds of 30-40kt; visibility was at times less than a quarter of a mile, and the average cloud ceiling of 1,000ft was frequently down to around

200ft. It says a lot for the crews that they found and attacked five enemy destroyers with 250lb and 20lb bombs, claiming hits on two. They also reported six merchant ships and logged the positions of sunken ships, mines and shore batteries. Six Swordfish were damaged and two ditched in the sea. At 17.05hrs 816 Squadron was launched to have another try, but the weather this time was even worse and the raid was aborted.

On 13 April a major naval action was fought in what became known as the Second Battle of Narvik. It was during early morning that *Warspite*, flying the flag of Vice-Adm W. J. Whitworth KCB, DSO, passed through the entrance of Ofot Fiord, screened by nine destroyers. Narvik lay 30 miles up the fiord with a strong German naval force of destroyers in the area. *Furious* flew off an anti-submarine patrol ahead of the British ships and arranged a strike force of 10 Swordfish for a possible synchronised attack. In spite of the

Far left:
In a scene that could be described as typically Norway, Swordfish peel off for a dive bombing attack. *J. Bryant*

Above left:
Swordfish taking off from *Furious*. Her aircraft were in constant action during the Norwegian campaign. *G. T. A. Darley*

Left:
The rain-lashed deck of *Furious* in another view such as might have been seen off Norway. Note the bombs under the wings and the deck crews faithfully at the chocks. *G. T. A. Darley*

adverse weather the strike force arrived at its predetermined time and dive-bombed from 2,000ft through a partial clearance in the clouds. Thirty-five 250lb and 70 20lb bombs were dropped but no hits were made, and two Swordfish were lost due to enemy action.

However, it was the action of a single Swordfish floatplane that day which changed the course of the action. Petty Officer F. C. Rice, with Lt-Cdr W. L. M. Brown as observer and Leading Airman M. G. Pacey as TAG, was the pilot of Swordfish L9767 launched from *Warspite* at 11.52hrs to spot for the force. The cloud base was actually down to the cliff-tops on each side of the fiord, forming a dirty canopy, and as the Swordfish slowly flew up the fiord the observer remarked that 'it was like flying up a tunnel'. Fortunately, overcast visibility had improved to about six miles.

A German destroyer, the *Kunne*, was the first ship to be spotted by the approaching force, but in the face of superior numbers it withdrew up the fiord. A second destroyer, the *Kollner*, was in no position to offer battle so headed for Djupvik Bay on the south side of the fiord, where its captain set up an ambush. The Swordfish observed this around 12.40hrs and reported it to the flagship. Dashing in, the leading British destroyers, *Bedouin* and *Eskimo*, both achieved hits with torpedoes before the enemy could even get one salvo away, and within three

minutes the *Kollner* was ablaze fore and aft; *Warspite's* guns finished her off shortly afterwards. Pressing on, Petty Officer Rice flew into Herjangs Fiord, which lies north of Narvik. There he observed an enemy submarine, the *U64*, at anchor some 50yd from the jetty at Bjerkvik. Rice dived to 300ft to release two 350lb bombs, the first hitting the bows; owing to the explosion it was difficult to see exactly where the other fell. The TAG, Pacey, raked the conning tower with machine gun fire, but the Germans, quick off the mark, got in some return shots which damaged the tailplane of the Swordfish, making it sluggish on the controls. For the rest of the patrol Rice had to handle the aircraft very carefully. The *U64* sank within 30 seconds, and was the first U-boat sunk in World War 2 by an aircraft — and an obsolescent biplane, relatively lightly armed, at that. (Swordfish went on to sink 12½ enemy U-boats during the war, and shared in the destruction of eight others.) The observer, Lt-Cdr Brown, had also been able to warn the advancing force of five torpedo tracks approaching, which allowed the ships to take avoiding action: the torpedoes exploded harmlessly against the cliffs.

Narvik lies near the entrance to Rombaks Fiord and three enemy destroyers were observed moving along it under a smoke screen. Moving up, the British ships overwhelmed the *Giese* and *Roeder* at Narvik, setting them on fire. The British destroyers then raced on, with the Swordfish overhead repor-

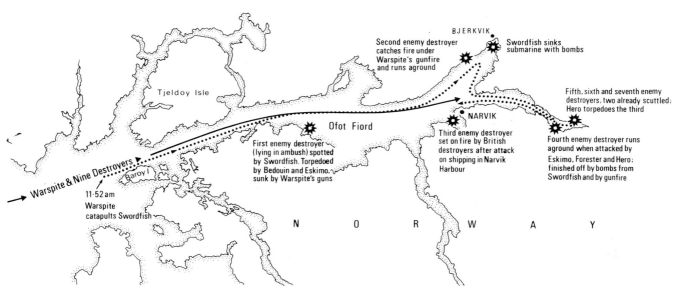

Second enemy destroyer
catches fire under
Warspite's gunfire
and runs aground

BJERKVIK

Swordfish sinks
submarine with bombs

Tjeldoy Isle

Fifth, sixth and seventh enemy
destroyers, two already scuttled;
Hero torpedoes the third

Ofot Fiord

NARVIK

Third enemy destroyer
set on fire by British
destroyers after attack
on shipping in Narvik
Harbour

Fourth enemy destroyer runs
aground when attacked by
Eskimo, Forester and Hero;
finished off by bombs from
Swordfish and by gunfire

First enemy destroyer
(lying in ambush) spotted
by Swordfish. Torpedoed
by Bedouin and Eskimo,
sunk by Warspite's guns

Warspite & Nine Destroyers

Baroy I

11·52 am
Warspite
catapults Swordfish

N   O   R   W   A   Y

ting the enemy positions. At 15.00hrs
the *Eskimo* engaged two enemy destroyers only to lose her bow to a torpedo,
but by then *Forrester* and *Hero* had
opened fire and a German destroyer ran
aground, to be finished off by gunfire
and by bombs from the Swordfish.
Warspite was engaging the enemy at
distance, but smoke from her exploding
shells combined with low clouds, sleet or
snow and the steepness of the cliffs on
either side of the narrow fiord, made
flying and observation very hazardous.

It was around this time that Petty
Officer Rice dropped out of the action for
a short time, a hitherto unrecorded
event. Lt-Cdr Rice reveals that:

'During the Second Battle of Narvik, as
the cloud was too low, we could not do
any spotting, so we landed in a small
bay down the fiord. A couple of Norwegian fishermen took Brown and myself
ashore in a small boat to the local post
office. We left poor old Pacey to guard
the floatplane with a .45 revolver. We
then made a 'phone call to an
Englishman on the other side of the
fiord. I gave some chocolate to the
children at the post office as we always
carried some because in those days no

21

Right:
The flight deck of _Ark Royal_, the Swordfish of which made a valuable contribution in the Norwegian conflict.
Cdr R. N. Everett

Below:
Seen from Swordfish floatplane L9767 is a German destroyer beached against the snow-covered rocks of Herjangs Fiord.
IWM (A36)

Bottom:
The British destroyer _Hero_ after being torpedoed during the Second Battle of Narvik. The flak-damaged tailplane of the Swordfish can be discerned in this view. *IWM (A9809)*

flying rations were issued. After about an hour the gunfire in the fiord had eased so we decided to take-off and go back to the ship.'

At 15.30hrs _Bedouin_ signalled that three enemy destroyers were located in positions that gave them an advantage for a torpedo attack. Vice-Adm Whitworth remarked:
'The torpedo menace must be accepted. Enemy must be destroyed without delay. Take _Kimberley_, _Hero_, _Forrester_ and _Punjabi_ under your orders and organise attack, sending most serviceable destroyer first. Ram or board if necessary.' However, when the destroyer force moved up the fiord it found the enemy had abandoned their ships, two (_Zenker_ and _Arnim_) being scuttled, one (_Thiele_) sinking, and another (_Ludemann_) sent to the bottom by a torpedo from _Hero_. The main action was over, and the Swordfish floatplane returned to _Warspite_ after being in the air for four hours. During that time, under extremely difficult conditions, it had reported enemy positions — thus allowing British ships the tactical advantage — fall of shot and torpedo tracks, taken photographs, bombed a destroyer and sunk a U-boat: not a bad day's work for an old biplane. In his despatch Vice-Adm Whitworth said, 'The enemy reports made by _Warspite's_ aircraft were invaluable. I doubt if ever a shipborne aircraft has been used to such good purpose as it was in this operation'. Petty Officer Rice received a

Left:
Taken from the Swordfish floatplane, this photo shows the jetty and, in the background, the local post office where Petty Officer Rice made his call and sent postcards. *Lt-Cdr F. C. Rice*

Bottom:
The battleship *Warspite*, seen from the Swordfish returning to the ship after the Narvik action. Note the ship's crane already out to accept the aircraft.
Lt Cdr F. C. Rice

well-earned DSM and Lt-Cdr Brown a DSC, but the TAG, Pacey, received nothing! This was fairly typical of the official attitude towards awards for air gunners at that time, and although the TAG remained an essential part of Fleet Air Arm aircrew until well after the war, the attitude did not change.

The Home Fleet returned to Scapa Flow on 15 April but *Furious* remained behind to support the land forces. Her Swordfish were constantly airborne, attacking targets ashore and afloat in the Narvik area, bombing destroyers and jetties, and carrying out anti-submarine and photographic reconnaissance patrols; once nine Swordfish bombed enemy transport aircraft parked on a frozen lake. Flying was extremely hazardous because of enemy fighters, steep mountains, no proper maps, and abysmal weather, usually with prolonged snow or sleet squalls, and fog. Aircrews frequently returned frozen through, but still had to land on to a pitching and slush-covered flight deck in winds up to 50kt. The Commanding Officer of *Furious*, Capt T. H. Troubridge, wrote:

'It is difficult to speak without emotion of the pluck and endurance of the young officers and men, some of them Midshipmen, who flew their aircraft to such good effect . . . All were firing their first shots in action, whether torpedo, bomb or machine gun; many made their first night landing on 11 April, and, undeterred by the loss of several of their shipmates, their honour and courage remained throughout as dazzling as the snow-covered mountain over which they so triumphantly flew.'

When *Furious* was relieved on 25 April she had only eight serviceable Swordfish left and was far from being serviceable herself. Furthermore, a near-miss from a bomb dropped by a Heinkel bomber on 18 April had damaged her turbines so that she could only steam at a much reduced speed. Nevertheless, during the 14 days her Swordfish had flown 23,870 miles, fired 18 torpedoes, dropped 409 bombs and taken 295 photographs; some 17 Swordfish had been damaged by enemy action, nine being lost in the process with 12 casualties, three of them fatal. On 24 April *Ark Royal* and *Glorious* arrived from the Mediterranean and the following day *Furious* left Norwegian waters for the UK.

Below:
**Leading Seaman, later
Lieutenant-Commander,
F. C. Rice in the right
foreground, watching flying
training aboard *Courageous*
during January 1939.**
Flight International

Ark Royal's aircraft complement was 810 and 820 Squadrons with 12 Swordfish each, 800 Squadron with 12 Skuas, and 801 Squadron with six Skuas and six Rocs. *Glorious* had 823 Squadron with 12 Swordfish, 802 Squadron with 12 Sea Gladiators, 803 Squadron with six Skuas and 804 Squadron with six Sea Gladiators. The fighters immediately began to operate combat air patrols over the Army ashore while the Swordfish carried out daily strike and support duties. When *Ark Royal* withdrew on 28 April to replenish, her aircraft had accounted for nearly 40 enemy aircraft destroyed and damaged, for the loss of one Skua. *Glorious* arrived to fly off 18 RAF Gladiators of 263 Squadron to the frozen lake at Lesjaskou, after which she returned to Scapa Flow for another load. Within 48 hours all the RAF Gladiators were out of action.

Ark Royal returned on 4 May and stayed until 24 May, by which time *Furious* and *Glorious* had ferried out more Gladiators and some Hurricanes to be based at Bardufoss. It was during these hectic days of action that one Swordfish, piloted by Lt H. de G. Hunter, was ambushed by three enemy bombers. While his TAG, Leading Airman Bennett, fought them off with his Lewis, the observer, Lt A. W. N. Dayrell, signalled to *Ark Royal* 'From

Swordfish 4F, delayed by three Heinkels'. The following day, six Swordfish attacked the railway line east of Narvik. Taking two hours to fly there because of high winds, the strike force split up, one section going to bomb the Nordalshoen viaduct near the Swedish border, and the others overturning a train in Hunddallen railway station.

Furious returned on 21 May to fly off some more Gladiators, and *Glorious* followed a few days later with some Hurricanes. Narvik was at last taken on 28 May. But it was too late; the campaign in Norway was already lost and the battles being fought in the Low Countries were going badly for the Allies. The decision was made to withdraw the Allied forces and on 2 June *Ark Royal* and *Glorious* arrived off the Norwegian coast to cover the withdrawal. On 7 June three Hurricanes landed on *Glorious*, flown by RAF pilots with no previous deck-landing experience, proving that the Hurricane could be landed on a carrier and therefore be used as a fleet fighter. The remaining Hurricanes and Gladiators were flown aboard *Glorious* and she was detached from the Home Fleet to sail for Scapa Flow, escorted by the two destroyers *Ardent* and *Acasta*. Meanwhile the German battlecruisers *Scharnhorst* and *Gneisenau* were patrolling undetected between Jan Mayen Island and the Norwegian coast. About 180 miles west-northwest of the Lofoten Islands on the afternoon of 8 June, these large enemy ships sighted the *Glorious* and her escort. *Scharnhorst* opened fire at 16.30hrs at a range of 28,000yd and within 90 minutes the *Ardent* and *Glorious* had been sunk with the loss of 1,515 lives. *Acasta*, totally outclassed, gamely launched a torpedo attack on the *Scharnhorst* before she too was sunk. The attack was not in vain, however, for one torpedo damaged the big ship and she had to return to Trondheim to effect repairs. An attack by 15 Skuas of 800 and 803 Squadrons from *Ark Royal*, launched in broad daylight, was an unmitigated disaster, with eight of the aircraft being shot down.

The last action of 1940 around Norway was during September and October when *Furious* flew off Swordfish of 816 and 825 Squadrons to attack Tromso and Trondheim, the former being the first large-scale night torpedo attack carried out by the Fleet Air Arm — and nearly a month before the famous night attack on Taranto.

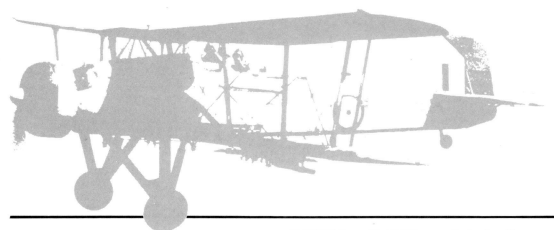

ATTACKED BY A DORNIER

The flying logbooks of aviators are quite often full of revealing and useful information to aviation historians, and those of the Fleet Air Arm are no exception. Take for instance an extract from Capt Ken Williamson's logbook for 11 November 1940: 'Attack on Taranto — failed to return'. What an understatement by the officer who led the first wave of Swordfish at Taranto! However, it is the entry in another logbook that caught my attention while researching this book: 'A/S patrol — attacked by Do215, 1 quarter and 5 stern attacks'. Surely here was an interesting tale? Cdr John Stenning, then a sub-lieutenant, recalls the day:

'I was serving with 821 Squadron at the time; in April we had disembarked from *Ark Royal* to Evanton, carrying out E- and U-boat searches off the Orkneys. In August we moved up to Hatston to carry out anti-submarine patrols around the Orkneys.

'On 23 October 1940, the day of the attack, I took off from Hatston in Swordfish L9743 at 07.15hrs to carry out an anti-submarine patrol to the southeast of Fair Isle at 1,000ft. I had Lt C. L. F. Webb as my observer and Leading Airman Craig as TAG. There we were cruising along looking for an enemy below, when he appeared from above! We certainly did not expect a German aircraft to be around and I seem to recall that when we first sighted it we thought it was a RAF kite. It approached from our starboard quarter and when the tracer came whizzing past I started avoiding action. This consisted of weaving, jinking and generally throwing the Swordfish about. He obviously thought our lumbering 90kt biplane was easy meat and came round for a stern attack. I quickly realised our only chance lay in staying low so I dived straight down over the sea and with throttle wide open — all of 120kt — headed for land. He made another attack and although my TAG was returning the fire he did not have much success because as soon as he opened fire I started jinking.

'He made four subsequent attacks from dead astern, firing the front guns on the approach, then, when nearly on us, turning away to starboard and letting the rear turret have a go. My observer, Charles Webb, shouted each time when to start taking avoiding action, and Craig, my TAG, had a go with our Lewis gun each time he came within range. After the sixth attack he gave up and flew away to the east — and I belted for Hatston!

'After landing we found a bullet in the radio, quite close to Webb and Craig, one of the interplane struts had been shot through, and there were some bullet holes in the wing fabric. I also realised that I had not even jettisoned my depth charges, which would have made it easier to throw the Swordfish about. I then thought that I could have dropped them as the Dornier came up astern and the column of water might have knocked him out of the sky — what a line that would have been — to have shot down a Dornier with depth charges!'

TECHNICAL NOTES

The Swordfish fuselage was a rectangular steel-tube structure made up in three parts joined together at the rear catapult spool and at the tailplane front spar. The structure was faired to an oval section with metal fairing panels attached to duralumin supports on the forward fuselage, with fabric-covered wooden panels covering the rear fuselage. A flotation bag with a buoyancy of 1,600lb filled the rear fuselage between stations J and K. The wings were of tubular steel spars, steel drag struts and duralumin ribs covered by fabric. The duralumin ailerons, one to each wing, were covered in fabric. A pyramid structure carried the upper centre section, with the lower centre section wing stubs braced to upper fuselage longerons by inverted V struts. The lower wing stubs and the upper centre section had metal covering to provide walkways. The interplane and undercarriage struts were faired to streamline section, but the centre section struts were left round. The undercarriage was anchored to the extremity of the front spars of the lower centre section, with lower end hinged to the fuselage by an axle and forwardly inclined radius rod.

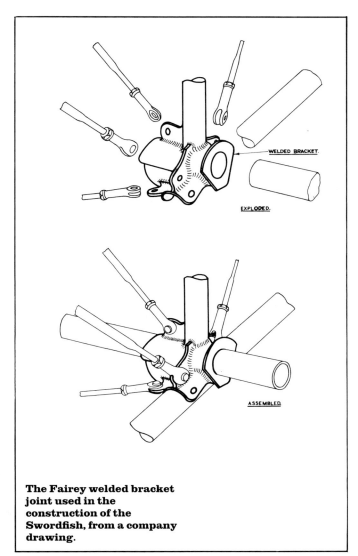

The Fairey welded bracket joint used in the construction of the Swordfish, from a company drawing.

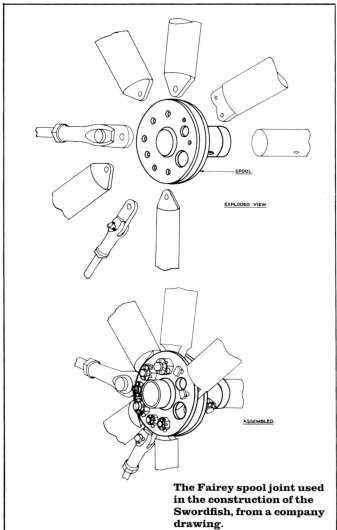

The Fairey spool joint used in the construction of the Swordfish, from a company drawing.

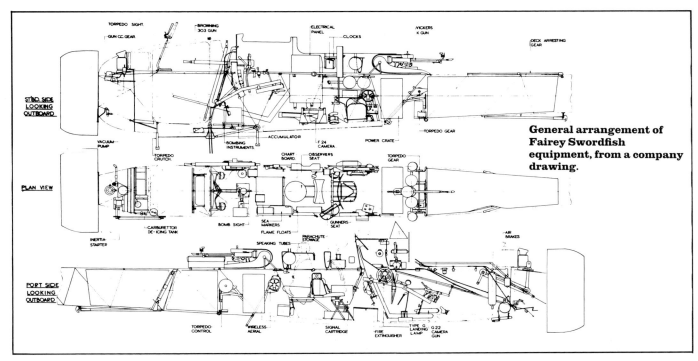

General arrangement of Fairey Swordfish equipment, from a company drawing.

In the legs was an oleo shock absorber, and the wheels, which were fully interchangeable with twin floats, had pneumatic brakes. The tail unit was made of steel and duralumin with fabric covering. Fixed armament consisted of one Vickers .303 machine gun mounted on the starboard upper front fuselage and firing through the airscrew, and a .303 Lewis gun was mounted in the rear cockpit on a Fairey high-speed gun mounting. Weapons arrangements that could be carried under the wings and fuselage were:

One 18in torpedo	1,610lb
Six 250lb and four 20lb bombs	1,580lb
Two 500lb, two 250lb and four 20lb bombs	1,580lb
Three 500lb bombs	1,500lb
One mine	1,500lb
Six 100lb bombs and eight 20lb bombs	760lb

The maximum permissible weapons load for catapult operations was 1,500lb, and loads on the Mk II and III Swordfish would vary when carrying four 60lb rocket projectiles under each wing.

The Swordfish's main fuel tank held 155gal and was located in the forward fuselage with a 12½gal gravity tank just forward of the pilot's instrument panel. An overload 69gal fuel tank could be fitted under the fuselage, but more often a 60gal tank was mounted on the upper longerons immediately behind the pilot in the rear cockpit. An extended hood with a windscreen could be placed over it, but it is doubtful whether this was very often fitted.

Early Mk I Swordfish were powered by the 690hp Bristol Pegasus IIIM3 nine-cylinder radial air-cooled engine. A Fairey-Reed metal airscrew was fitted and the engine was encased in a Townend ring cowling with a leading edge exhaust collector. Later production Swordfish had the more powerful Pegasus XXX rated at 750hp.

It was with this fabric-covered biplane that the Fleet Air Arm went to war, and it was still flying operationally when World War 2 ended. The flying side is recorded elsewhere, but what was involved when working on the Swordfish? Ex-rigger Tom Fagg recalls his nuts and bolts days:

'I was first introduced to the Swordfish as a very green AC1 metal rigger direct from tech training at No 4 School of

Top left:
A port side view showing the rear of the Pegasus engine, the inertia starter gearing and the fuel tank.

Centre left:
The cockpit area, with a Browning .303 machine gun in situ, used for mock-up purposes or to test the installation.

Bottom left:
The fuel tank forward of the cockpit and the struts to the stub planes.

Top right:
Here large panels are removed to show some of the rear cockpit area, including in the top left corner the spare drums of ammunition for the TAG Lewis gun.

Centre right:
A starboard view showing the W/T crate mounting and 12-volt accumulater stowage.

Bottom right:
The wing release mechanism that allowed the wings to fold back.

Technical Training at RAF Manston. This was around the end of July 1938 and my first posting was to Gosport, this then being a RAF station. As things turned out this was the period that, as we all know, became a rather hectic time prior to the war in 1939. My work in those days was mainly on major inspections and preparation of new aircraft ready for issue to operational units. When I joined Gosport a modification was being carried out on the Swordfish which changed all the bracing wires of the wings to stainless steel, along with their end shackles and locknuts. The wires, known as flying wires, landing wires or incidence wires, all have, when new, extra long threads at the right-hand threaded end. My job at this time was to cut the surplus off so as to have the wires at the required length for rigging the wings, or should I say, mainplanes. After a very short spell at Gosport, which included the "Munich panic", I moved to Kalafrana on Malta. Here I got more involved with the innards of the Swordfish, as they came from carriers and major ships for major inspections, the latter of course having floats. At Kalafrana the servicing area had no slipway, only deep water up to the sea wall. Swordfish, and other types, were flown in and taxied slowly under a crane jib; when the propeller had passed, the crane driver dropped the crane hook and a crewman on the Swordfish nipped the hook on to the aircraft centre section sling and the crane lifted it out the water and on to the apron. On one occasion I saw a most irate naval officer pilot as he spent half an hour taxying around in circles because the crane had cut out, preventing the driver from getting the jib into position for lifting; also, the crane was rotated away from the access ladder so the driver was marooned, hence a "blue cloud" around the bay! During my stay at Kalafrana the *Ark Royal* called in and on one occasion on its trip out from the UK some of her Swordfish had rather unfortunate landings on deck, which resulted in their being damaged. At Kalafrana we received at least two minus their wings, these having been cut off at the root. I understood this was done because of damage sustained and the need to clear the flight deck quickly, the offending wings being thrown overboard. The fuselage, still with engine and under-carriage, was lowered into the hangars until it could be left with a repair unit.

'It turned out that 18 to 20 Swordfish had been moved to Egypt during the 1938 Munich crisis and these were still in their packing cases at 102 MU at Abu Sueir. In April 1939 six of us airmen were dispatched to Abu Sueir to assemble these machines for issue to the Royal Navy. We soon ran into a technical snag: the normal practice to rig the wings was to adjust the bracing wires to what we knew as pin centre lengths. The wings were assembled on the hangar floor as port and starboard pairs (this was known as boxing the wings), and they were then lifted into position and attached by the wing bolts at top and bottom rear spar root positions, then spread to flight condition and the front locking lever actuated. Our snag was we had forgotten to take with us the list of bracing wire lengths so we had to rig the aircraft to set the correct incidence and dihedral of the wings using instruments. This done, we now attempted to fold the wings and found we could not withdraw the latches that locked them in the flight condition. The only answer was to adjust the various bracing wires until the latches were easy to latch and

Bottom:
The cowled Pegasus IIIM3 which time and again brought crews back when other engines would have given up the ghost. It was known for an engine to bring its crew home after two cylinders were shot away.

Right:
The business end — armourers load a torpedo into its cradle.

Far right:
A torpedo mounted under a Swordfish on Malta — note the spring.
Lt-Cdr R. E. F. Kerrison

Bottom right:
Trials were conducted with a searchlight mounted under the port wing and a generator under the centre fuselage, but it was not adopted — perhaps their Lordships felt the Stringbag was already lugging enough around!

SW. 40. SWORDFISH H.S. 553—ENCLOSED COCKPITS T.I. HOODINGS CLOSED.

unlatch, this being essential so that handlers on the carrier flight decks could fold wings and get aircraft down the lift to the hangars in the shortest possible time to keep the flight deck clear. This method of rigging was proven by flight testing with appropriate adjustment to the aileron trim, etc. Having got a successful flight, all the pin centres were measured and listed and the rest of the Swordfish were quickly assembled.

'The large dinghy which was stowed in the centre section needed to be treated with due care when being installed, a vacuum pump had to be used to evacuate all the air otherwise any air left could expand the dinghy with increasing aircraft altitude and it was possible for it to be ejected from its stowage — dangerous to say the least. The CO_2 bottle to inflate the dinghy was operated by water immersion switches, one low down on the undercarriage, and one on the engine bearers. If either of these were misaligned the slipstream could cause them to operate and inflate the dinghy. [It is interesting to note here that there were instances of dinghy releases in flight which could be highly

32

Above:
Rocket-Assisted Take-Off (RATO), which was so useful with a fully laden aeroplane, is seen here being tested on Swordfish NR995/G, the G indicating that the aircraft must be under guard when not flying. *IWM (A27683)*

Right:
The rear cockpit was designed for holding a navigator and air gunner with their associated equipment. Here an observer checks out his compasses prior to a flight.

Below right:
The strength of the structure was put to the test when this Swordfish, L9726 being piloted by an Air Transport Auxiliary pilot, flew into the Manchester area balloon barrage but managed to fly back to Ringway, Fairey's flight test aerodrome.
Lt Duncan Menzies

amusing or downright dangerous. On 4 May 1940 Lt Stenning was flying Swordfish P4143 of 821 Squadron when the dinghy suddenly released itself in level flight at 1,000ft. Lt Stenning says, "I do know that we had several similar incidents and as a result the wire cable attached from dinghy to aircraft was disconnected in all Swordfish so if you ditched you had to be very quick to grab the dinghy before it floated away."]

'On the subject of aircraft colours, prewar the aircraft were finished in silver dope but when war was declared an instruction was received to camouflage them. At this time there were two schemes, the colours mainly being sea-green and sea-grey, which were not in the same places on all aircraft. As an example, if you looked down on a formation the grey on one aircraft wing would merge in with the grey on the tailplane of another aircraft, giving no positive visual break and proving very dangerous in low light conditions. As this was in a bit of a panic we went to work at night to get the job done and recamouflage the aircraft. One airman's job was to repaint the roundels on the top wings, the white being omitted, and

Above:
The good old Peggy — the Bristol Pegasus IIIM3 which just kept on going whatever the weather or conditions. *Rolls-Royce*

the new roundel consisted of a dark red centre surrounded by a blue circle, except in this case when the airman suffered from a bit of colour blindness and in the poor light he painted blue centres with red circles.

'By now our original party of six had increased to about 50 and we were known as the Fleet Air Arm Light Repair Unit. Aircraft now started to come to us from operational units. A common "make do and mend" item was the Swordfish tailwheel tyre: we made discs of rubber clamped together when no proper replacement tyre was available — and they worked! Also at this time we found ourselves recovering wings and other fabric-covered areas. An airman fabric worker would machine the fabric into an open bag arrangement, then a couple of riggers would spend a fair amount of time

stitching the trailing edge of this cover plus all the cutouts for struts and wire attachments, then doping and stringing the fabric to the wing ribs. The flight controls of the Swordfish were runs of steel flexible cable, the longer runs being made up of two or three shorter lengths. This allowed for replacement of sections which ran around pulleys to be replaced when worn without the cost of a complete run. In many cases it was technically simpler to replace a section instead of a full run. New controls were usually made up by the rigger, this process consisting of splicing the cable around ferrules through which the attachment bolts were passed. As the cables had to be very accurate in length there needed to be a considerable amount of skill displayed by the rigger. The splice had to be tight and a good fit around the ferrules. I personally found splicing these cables at first made for sore hands but after a while one tended to develop hard hands where they came into contact with the cable during the tightening pull of the splice.

'At our level of maintenance we had very little to do with the torpedo, only the fitment of the crutch below the fuselage, complete with the securing cables and electric releases; also in the cockpit floor was a control which mated with the appropriate part of the torpedo for depth setting.

'Compared with modern aircraft engines the starting of the Pegasus was slow and laborious. The hand-cranked inertia starter, being highly geared, needed two men to get it up to speed before engaging it. And refuelling the Swordfish, at least at Abu Sueir, was a most time-consuming job. Fuel out there was supplied in four-gallon sealed cans and the sequence went something like this. The first man broke open the seal of each can and passed it to the next man who was stood on the wheel, and, using the undercarriage struts to assist his balance, he in turn passed the can to the third man who sat astride the front fuselage adjacent to the fuel filter cap. Fuel was then decanted into the tank using a large funnel which had a chamois leather fitted as a filter. In the Middle East at least, when the leather gathered the sand and dirt, it restricted the flow of fuel into the tank — as a result it could take all morning just to fill up two Swordfish by this method.

'Occasionally we got the opportunity to fly, usually on a pass-off test or an air-test. Now, when one flew in the centre and rear cockpits the safety device was a steel cable attached to the floor structure, the other end having a special catch which attached to the lower part of the parachute harness. Our RAF test pilot would only take passengers in the Swordfish when this device was fitted, and so long as they were engine or airframe fitters. He did not have much experience on the Swordfish and flew it very soberly so when the opportunity arose to go on a flight test two of us asked to go along — the cables not being fitted as none were available. Climbing to a safe height we found the pilot had in fact become accustomed to the aeroplane and proceeded to throw it around the sky — with a pair of idiots in the rear cockpit hanging on to fuselage struts and the general structure to prevent being thrown out as the pilot pulled it up until it was hanging on the prop and doing stall turns, etc.

'Towards the end of 1940 I was moved from the Fleet Air Arm unit which was transferred to Fayid and came under full naval command, and became deeply involved in keeping aircraft in repair for our desert air force.'

Above:
A diving Swordfish firing rockets. The fitting of rockets to the Swordfish opened up a whole new chapter in its history, and the concept was proven when a submarine was sunk by a lone Swordfish on patrol. *IWM (A23784)*

Below:
The Portuguese government granted the Allies facilities in the Azores to respond to the U-boat danger to convoys. Until the arrival of RAF units with Flying Fortresses and Hudsons, the task was fulfilled by the Fleet Air Arm with escort carriers. Here, showing the typical conditions under which they operated when ashore, a Swordfish is refuelled from jerry cans by RAF groundcrew. *IWM (CA38)*

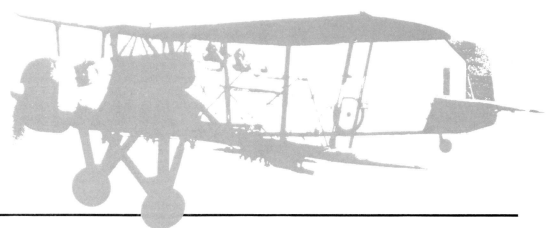

TRIUMPH AT TARANTO

'My first intimation of the Taranto attack was a cryptic note on the blackboard in the starboard for'd corner of No 1 hangar in *Illustrious* which said "BLITZ ON TARANTO",' recalls Lt-Cdr E. W. Whitley. He was to remember it for the rest of his life.

The Fleet Air Arm plan to attack the Italian fleet in Taranto harbour had been conceived as far back as 1935 using the three TBR squadrons, 812, 823 and 825, aboard HMS *Glorious*. This plan, one of a number drawn up at the time, was responsible for a large quantity of prewar naval aircrew being given extensive training in all aspects of delivering a warload by air while operating from carriers within striking distance of their target. However, when the war did break out, *Glorious* was required to support the Norwegian campaign and sailed to join the Home Fleet on 10 April 1940. Nevertheless, the original plan was dusted off and revised for an attack coinciding with Trafalgar Day, 21 October 1940. Thirty Swordfish were to make the attack in two waves of 15 aircraft, nine aircraft of each wave carrying torpedoes and six carrying bombs. *Illustrious*, the first of the new class of armoured carrier, was sent to the Mediterranean to replace *Glorious*. She had up to 4in of flight deck armour, armoured wall and hangar deck and was fitted with RDF (radar). She carried 815 and 819 Squadrons equipped with Swordfish and 806 Squadron with the new Fulmar fighter. Lt-Cdr Whitley joined *Illustrious* prior to joining the Mediterranean Fleet and it is interesting

to read of this and his views on carrier deck life before and during the Taranto action:

'I was a RAF apprentice at Halton, starting in January 1937 with the 35th entry. Early in 1939 I transferred to the Fleet Air Arm and on passing out went to the clearance camp at Puckpool on the Isle of Wight. In January 1940 I was sent to join 819 Squadron at Ford with three other young air fitters. I was most disappointed to find I was to work on Swordfish as the training had been on Spitfires and Blenheims. The squadron was made up of 12 pilots, 12 observers, 12 TAGs, 12 AM(E), 12 AM(A), along with some electricians, armourers, store bashers and the like. The pilots and observers were all "straight" navy, the NCOs were RAF and the mechanics mostly ex-seamen and stokers who had changed horses as we had. Before we ex-brats had had time to get used to the idea of these antique aeroplanes we had our second chastening experience — we were not allowed to touch them — it was our job to run the petrol bowsers with their wrist-breaking Lister engines . . . three years technical training to be a garage attendant! Eventually, of course, we were let loose on the aircraft, painting the squadron letters on the side and applying lanolin to bracing wires.

'The squadron [CO was Lt-Cdr J. W. "Daddy" Hale] worked up at Ford and at Easter 1940 we went to West Freugh for armament practice. There was much bombing and gunnery practice. I remember the aircraft dinghies arriving

and spending the Easter weekend packing 12, one to each aircraft. The first took five hours, the last just 55 minutes! The only light moment was when a CO_2 bottle was inadvertently released and zoomed off round the hangar like a berserk black bee . . . fortunately without damaging anything. The first of my many Swordfish flights was at West Freugh, a series of climbs up to 10,000ft and dives on to a target in Luce Bay. I tried to watch but the "G" on pullout defeated me and I spent that part of all the subsequent dives on the cockpit floor. At the end of camp we flew back to Ford, taxying in near Sir Alan Cobham's hangars at the Yapton side of the aerodrome. In May, Wilf Jones, my opposite number, and I flew up to Speke with Lts Garten-Stone and Skelton for some initial deck trials. A new and mysterious aircraft at Speke turned out to be a Fulmar and all three aircraft were towed to Gladstone Dock with frequent stops to grease the wheel bearings which were not designed for such long journeys. Here they were lifted on board by a dockside crane, the Swordfish having sling hooks built into the centre section. It was around 25 May 1940 that we ranged the aircraft and I started up Swordfish L5L [an 819 Squadron aircraft] with Lt Garten-Stone yelling for me to get in. Now, before leaving Ford, the CO had said "Ballast the aircraft for deck trials and don't fly in it". I explained this to the pilot, but he was adamant, he was a lieutenant, I was an air fitter, I got in. It was very early in the morning, so no breakfast, not even a cup of tea. Clad in a pair of blue overalls and no flying helmet I was quickly treated to a stomach-churning sight of rows of ships steaming up or down hill depending on where Lt Garten-Stone was throwing the aeroplane. The slipstream was cold so I tied my scarf round my head to cover my ears; the goofers on *Illustrious* must have thought we had landed at Fleetwood and picked up a fishwife! Eventually we approached the ship and I braced myself for an entirely new experience — but the real thing was an anti-climax, the arrested landing surprisingly gentle on what I believe was the first landing on *Illustrious*. Apparently on the way to Greenock some engineless Swordfish were fired off the catapult to test it — but much to the consternation of some local fishing boats.

'After the trials we flew back to the squadron, now at Roborough near Plymouth, and the ship steamed to Devonport. In June we sailed for Bermuda for the ship's shakedown but ran into dreadful weather which tore off all of the fifteen hundred feet or so of copper bar which was the degaussing loop. After the cruise it was back to John Brown's yard at Clydebank for new degaussing and other minor repairs. After a few days' leave we sailed to join the Eastern Mediterranean Fleet, passing Pantelleria on the first anniversary of the start of the war. They were exciting times: the squadron flew anti-submarine patrols from dawn to dusk, which gave the fitters a long day, especially when we changed roles to bomb targets in the Greek Islands or North Africa. On return to harbour we inevitably had to fit the heavy target towing winch for gunnery practice. Normally the Fleet was based at Alexandria and when in harbour the squadrons disembarked to Dekheila.

'At one stage someone had the idea of carrying a full-size depth charge on the Swordfish. I hit on the idea of a couple of strips of angle iron from the adjusting screws on the torpedo rack with the steadying pads moved to suit the length of the charge. The torpedo gunner ran up a strip of metal bent down at the ends to locate the charge fore and aft with a block welded on to match the one on the torpedo. The slings used to support and release the torpedo were still used. This device was flogged around the Med for ages; the only time it was used the charge failed to go off and the sub surfaced and put a few rounds through

Above:
A RAF reconnaissance picture of Taranto harbour taken just before the raid.
IWM (C3254)

37

the Swordfish! The squadron also laid magnetic mines, and the raids on the desert targets used bombs with a long extension on the nose to achieve an explosion before they buried themselves in the sand. With torpedoes I had the job of winding 21½ft of wire on to two spools and setting up the drum control gear which, together with the air tail, controlled the torpedo's angle on release. I did this later for all the Swordfish dropping torpedoes at Taranto.

'The Swordfish took a fearful bashing at sea; for instance, gun blast caused damage to the fabric-covered wings and fuselage and we lost bits overboard if we were careless. When being ranged on deck with heavily-loaded wings folded back it created havoc with the tyres, as

did the constant crossing of wires. When our stocks of spares were used up we made makeshift ones with rubber discs cut from the old mainwheel tyres. The Swordfish had their minor inspections at 30 hours, which meant every week, and a major at 120 hours, which came around once every four or five weeks. In those days we were forever tired. Eventually came those three words on the blackboard — BLITZ ON TARANTO — with the list of aircraft and what loads they were to carry. By the morning of the attack all was ready. As I mentioned earlier it was my task to wind and set the gear in the Swordfish that controlled the angle of drop of the torpedo. The 21½ft of wire was wound by hand on to a pair of spools about three inches in diameter. These spools fitted on to a shaft which ran across the

fuselage behind the gunner's cockpit. The shaft was damped with lead weights on a flange and wound against a spring. The free ends of the cable were attached to the air tail on the torpedo which held back the tail as it was released, thus setting up the correct angle. The importance of this set-up is obvious when I tell you that to drop the torpedo the aircraft has to be at 150ft and in level flight with no deviations and requiring five fathoms of water or more.

'It was on the morning of the raid that we had another setback. A Swordfish from 819 Squadron flown by Sub-Lt Alistair Keith with Lt George Going as observer took-off for a routine anti-submarine patrol but as they climbed away the engine died and they had to ditch. Both were OK and were picked up by the cruiser Gloucester. We had a serious problem, 819 had lost three Swordfish in three days due to engine failure. Water was suspected so one of the 819 aircraft had the fuel tanks drained and checked. Inside was water, sand and a peculiar growth not unlike seaweed. There was no option but to drain and refill every aircraft on board, including five extra Swordfish flown aboard Illustrious for the attack. The fuel tank drains are inside a panel over the torpedo rack; this meant that all aircraft ranged with torpedoes would have to have them removed. To ensure that all the fuel, and, more importantly, all the water, was drained, the aircraft had to be put in the flying position. This required the tails to be lifted — with the wings folded — so bombs and flares had to be removed too. It was a case of all hands to the pump, whoever was available was called in to help lift aircraft tails, drag bombs, move torpedoes, jacking equipment, etc, even the aircrews helped, which was hardly the thing to do with a difficult night operation ahead. Eventually, somehow we did it, with the aircraft all drained, filters checked, carbs drained, pipes checked, everything replaced and the aircraft refuelled through chamois leathers. We made it. The first wave was ranged ready.

'Ranging aircraft on a flight deck at night was a hair-raising experience. Initially you had no night vision, and as the gun crews pushed the aircraft aft one checked position by counting two barriers and six wires after which you knew there was the aft lift, "up" one hoped, then the round-down and then the long drop to the sea. Another

Above:
Bombs for the Swordfish of 815 and 819 Squadrons lined up on the flight deck of *Illustrious* — the nearest one reads, 'Next stop — Taranto'.

interesting little snag was that if you pushed on the interplane struts of the folded wing the following wheel often caught an ankle and produced a fracture! I believe that the true worth of the flight deck crews has never been really appreciated and I hope that these few words may redress the balance somewhat!

'Aircraft were manned, started up and as each aircraft taxied to the centre line for take-off we spread the wings and hopped off, leaving it to the Flight Deck Officer to wave them away. All the first wave got away successfully. We ranged the second wave, same thing, but after the seventh Swordfish took off the next two taxied forward together and met. The metal slat on the leading edge of one aircraft made a considerable hole in the wing of the other. In those days we had no protective headgear and I had blonde hair. If ever the FDO wanted anything it was easy to yell "Whitley" if he could see that hair. He didn't waste words, "Can they go?" he yelled. I pointed to the one with the small dent in the slat, "That one can, the other can't", I replied. There was no argument; I had the last word. As we pushed the damaged Swordfish to the for'd lift, its pilot, Lt Clifford, and his observer, Lt Going, ran past towards the island. They had gone to get permission to go on the strike if the aircraft could be repaired in time, I thought they were mad! One wave would have already stirred up a hornet's nest, another was following and they would be half an hour after that. We got the aircraft below, the internal structural members and bracing of the wing were intact so we pushed in the broken ribs and doped a huge patch over the hole. The dope dried almost instantly in the heat of the hangar so the aircraft was ranged again very quickly and the crew took-off on their lonely flight. We settled down to wait.

'Surprisingly, it wasn't long before we were piped to land on one aircraft. This was another interesting job at night . . . the aircraft approached with nav lights on so bats could see them, then as soon as he got the "cut" they were switched off. It they caught the wire they eventually appeared as dark shapes, we folded the wings and struck them down before the next landed on. If they missed the wire the next thing seen was a Stringbag at full chat as he took-off again. The aircraft returning was that of Lt Sam Morford. Apparently one of the straps holding the long-range fuel tank had snapped with the other giving way a few seconds later. Lt Morford's Swordfish was the one slightly damaged on the flight deck which I had allowed to go in the second wave. Approaching the carrier they had failed to give the correct colours of the day and gun crews on *Illustrious* opened up on them. Fortunately they weren't hit and landed on safely shortly afterwards. As the blinking identification signals of each returning Swordfish spelled out the aircraft letter and the dark shapes landed on we could hardly believe it . . . all accounted for bar two, nineteen out of twenty-one, relief flooded through the ship and with it the feeling of having achieved a major victory.'

The raid on Taranto was a magnificent and timely victory that will forever be a classic to the students of naval warfare. It was magnificent in that although the attack was a success it had come as no surprise to the Italians who had been on the alert for such an action: the success says much for the planning and leadership of the raid. And it was timely because Britain was going through a depressing phase of defeats and air attacks on her capital, and the electrifying effect of the news was incalculable to the British and her allies at that time. But what of the attack? The leader of the first strike, Lt-Cdr K. Williamson, gives his own assessment of the situation prior to the attack and his own part in it: '21 October 1940, Trafalgar Day, was the date originally selected for the attack, but for various reasons it had to be put off until 11 November — an equally auspicious date in our history. Previous to this the RAF had carried out a series of reconnaissances from Malta, and their excellent photographs showed that on the morning of 11 November there were five battleships, two of which were of the modern "Littorio" class, and three cruisers in the outer harbour. In the inner harbour there were more cruisers and destroyers. On the afternoon of 11 November the RAF reported that the sixth and last Italian battleship was approaching Taranto. So on that night the entire Italian fleet would be obligingly just where we wanted them. It was clear from the very start of the war with Italy that the Italians had no intention of risking their fleet in a general action with ours. From their point of view this was undoubtedly the correct strategy. As long as they had a "fleet in being" in the central Mediterranean area it constituted a permanent menace to our communications and compelled us to keep powerful forces always ready to deal with possible raids in strength on our convoys. In fact, the Italians in 1940 had nothing to gain and everything to lose if they risked their battleships in a fleet action.

'From our point of view, of course, the sooner this threat was eliminated, the better. If the enemy wouldn't come to us, then we would have to go to him — even if it meant attacking him inside his well-defended home ports. This could only be done from the air, and Rear-Adm Lyster, who then commanded the Mediterranean aircraft carriers, was convinced that the Fleet Air Arm could do the job. The idea of sinking an enemy fleet in harbour was not new to any of us, for years before the war the Royal Navy's torpedo bomber squadrons had practised this form of attack, and for years the gunnery experts had maintained that no aircraft would ever be able to get close enough to drop its torpedoes before being shot down. The introduction of the multiple pom-pom strengthened this belief, but the pilots still felt that a good proportion of aircraft would get through and drive their attack home. Events at Taranto proved them to be right.

'Taranto itself has a well-defined outer and inner harbour, like many ports. The outer harbour is roughly in the shape of a half moon running north and south. The inner harbour is joined to the outer harbour at the top, or northern tip, by a narrow channel. The Italian battleships lay in the outer harbour close to the shore in the centre of this half moon, protected on the south by a long mole and further to the north by three cruisers, which were most inconveniently moored behind nets right in the middle of the best line of approach for our visiting Swordfish aircraft. Close examination of our aerial photographs — and you can guess how we pored over them — revealed a large number of spots about the size of a small pinhead, which the experts pronounced to be barrage balloons. They were mostly on the land to the east of the anchorage, and as we intended to approach from the west, their presence was not unduly alarming — except that they might perhaps get in the way of a possible line of retreat after the attack. What was disconcerting though, was that there appeared to be a number of balloons about three hundred yards

apart all along the mole from the south, and another bunch of balloons flying from buoys or rafts on the seaward, or west side, of the three cruisers. It was decided that the best approach lanes for the torpedo-carrying aircraft were the two tips of the half moon, and there didn't seem to be much to choose between them. The northern route involved flying a little further close to the shore and passing nearer to the cruisers, whereas the southern approach meant that the aircraft would have to fly through the barrage balloons on the mole. These, as I have said, were spaced about three hundred yards apart, but we felt that as the span of a Swordfish was a little less than sixteen yards the chances were in our favour of passing through without hitting anything. I did in fact pass through them, and for a long time afterwards my observer, Lt Scarlett, was kind enough to consider that I had shown great skill in avoiding them. In the end, however, I was forced to disillusion him — I never even saw a balloon! We had two squadrons of Swordfish on the aircraft carrier *Illustrious* in 1940 — 815 and 819. Each squadron normally had nine aircraft, but early in November 1940, 819 Squadron had the bad luck to lose two which had force-landed in the sea. To make up for this, and add to the strength of the attack, five Swordfish were borrowed from *Eagle*. So *Eagle* shared the action with *Illustrious*. Three of these reinforcements were allotted to 815 Squadron, bringing its strength to 12 aircraft, and the other two were lent to 819 Squadron to replace its two losses.

'For this night attack both squadrons were to fly in three sub-flights variously armed. 815 Squadron was to start half an hour before 819, so that there would be really two attacks, with a half hour interval between them.

'I must make it clear that not all the aircraft in either squadron carried torpedoes, because, in order to give the torpedo aircraft a better chance to drive their attacks right home, it was thought best to stage some diversionary bombing a minute or two before. As well as this, of course, since it was a night attack, we had to carry flares to light up our real torpedo targets — the battleships.

'So, both squadrons when they arrived at Taranto were to act like this — as soon as the leader of the squadron was abreast of the southern tip of the

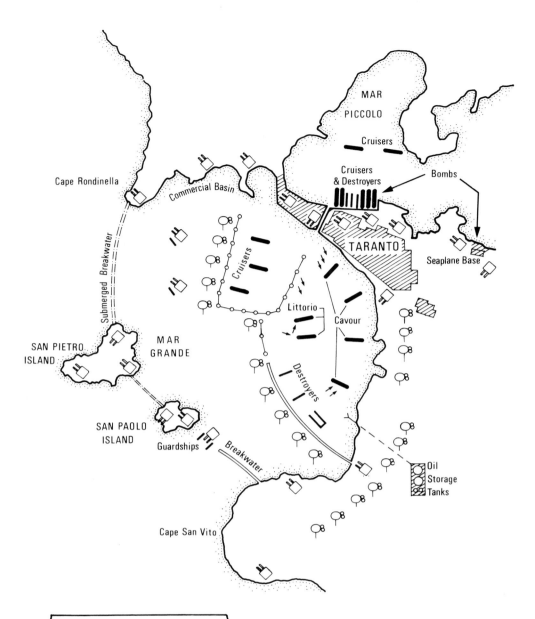

MAR
PICCOLO

Cruisers

Cruisers
& Destroyers

Bombs

Cape Rondinella

Commercial Basin

TARANTO

Seaplane Base

Submerged Breakwater

Cruisers

SAN PIETRO
ISLAND

MAR
GRANDE

Littorio

Cavour

SAN PAOLO
ISLAND

Destroyers

Guardships

Breakwater

Oil
Storage
Tanks

Cape San Vito

A A Batteries
Balloon Barrage
Net Defences
Torpedo Dropping Positions
Floating Dock

entrance to the outer harbour, he would
detach two flare droppers. They were to
fly behind the enemy battleships, drop
their flares and light the battleships up.
At the same time the sub-flight who
carried bombs only were to go full speed
— about 100 knots — for the inner
harbour. This was in the hope of
making the enemy think that the main
attack was being made on the lesser fry
— the cruisers and destroyers which

were anchored there. This attack was to
be under way before the torpedo aircraft
went in at low level. The torpedo aircraft
were to delay slightly and then make a
double attack, half from the southern
tip of the outer harbour, and the other
half from the northern tip. In this way
the battleships were to be attacked from
both sides at once. So you see, the theory
was that the bombers would create such
a diversion that the torpedo aircraft
would be able to sneak in, deliver their
attack, and get away unobserved. 819
Squadron was to repeat this surprise
half an hour later. When I propounded
this theory to my squadron, I am afraid
they greeted it with a considerable
amount of ribald merriment.

'There was great activity in the
hangar that evening. Each aeroplane
had its own maintenance crew, and
every crew was more than usually

Above:
**Taranto harbour,
11 November 1940.**

anxious that nothing should go wrong with any part of the aircraft. One of the Swordfish of 815 Squadron had been badly damaged as a result of a heavy landing on the deck two days previously, and teams of riggers had worked on it continuously since then in a feverish endeavour to get it ready in time for the raid. I can well remember the sergeant rigger's tired, triumphant, dirty face when he reported the aircraft fully serviceable about an hour before it was due to be ranged. He had been working more or less continuously for about 36 hours.

'The torpedoes, bombs and flares were brought into the hangar at about six o'clock and not long afterwards all was ready. The steel warheads of the torpedoes were covered with a thin film of oil, which gave the wags an opportunity to inscribe suitable messages on them, such as "To Musso from Minnie", "Best wishes from Illustrious" — to which somebody had added very properly, "and Eagle".

'At eight o'clock the 12 Swordfish of 815 Squadron were ranged on deck, and the ship was about 170 miles from Taranto. Rear-Adm Lyster and Capt Boyd wished the crews the best of luck, and shortly after half past eight the squadron was airborne and we were heading for the target. 819 Squadron was then ranged on deck and took-off half an hour after 815 had left. One of their aircraft was slightly damaged whilst manoeuvring on deck, but it was quickly repaired — while the crew sought and readily obtained permission from Capt Boyd to take off by themselves about 20 minutes after the rest had gone.

'The leading squadron — 815 — climbed steadily at about 75kt until they reached 7,500ft and then settled down on the course for Taranto at 90kt. This was a comfortable speed for the pilot to fly at, and it also simplified the observer's problem as 90 knots is 1½ nautical miles a minute. Unkind pilots used to say that any other speed would completely fox the observer, but that's gross libel! On the way up to our height we passed through a thin layer of cloud at about 4,000ft, and unfortunately the four bomber Swordfish became detached. They proceeded independently to Taranto arriving there shortly before the main body, but this in no way affected the outcome, as once the Italians opened up their barrage fire it covered the whole area anyway — and

so, as we had all suspected, there never was any chance of our torpedo aircraft attacking unopposed.

'It was at about 11 o'clock, when we were still about eight miles short of the target, that the bombers went in. There suddenly appeared ahead the most magnificent firework display I have ever seen. The whole area was full of red and blue bullets which rose to a height of about 8,000ft. These were incendiary and explosive bullets, but there were also armour-piercing bullets mixed with them which fortunately we couldn't see! At this point, Lt Scarlett, my observer, who hadn't spoken a word for the last hour and a half, suddenly said "There's Taranto". I thanked him, and we both agreed that the reception committee appeared to be extremely wide awake.

'As we approached the southern tip of the half moon the two flare droppers were detached and the two torpedo aircraft on the port side of the leading sub-flight fell back astern of the leader. These three torpedo aircraft then turned in and headed for the southern portion of the battlefleet. A few moments later the other torpedo-carrying sub-flight, led by Lt Kemp, turned to the east and approached the enemy ships along the northern tip of the half moon — all according to plan. We had to fly low for about 3½ miles through the barrage, and there was something morbidly attractive about those bullets. They appeared to approach very slowly until they were just short of the aircraft, then they suddenly accelerated and whistled past, if you were lucky, at whatever speed bullets do whistle past. For the pilot this is all very exciting and not unduly alarming, as all pilots as a race have an extraordinary and totally unjustifiable belief in their own personal immortality. The observer, however — a reasonable type — doesn't share this sublime faith, and for him it must be rather like being a passenger in a car without any brakes, which is careering down a steep hill with a learner driver at the wheel. And worse, all the observer could do after he had brought the pilot to the target area was to crouch at the bottom of a totally unarmoured open cockpit with a still partially filled long-range petrol tank, shaped like an inverted U, immediately over his head.

'All the torpedo aircraft reached the battlefleet, and all, skimming over the water, dropped their torpedoes from heights varying between thirty and fifteen feet above the surface. Just about then the short-range anti-aircraft fire was intense, and as every bullet has to come to rest sooner or later, I've often wondered how many finished up in the town and dockyard. In the meantime the bombers and flare droppers were bombing ships in the inner harbour, the three cruisers to seaward of the battleships, a seaplane base and some oil storage tanks.

'I doubt if any of the aircraft were under fire for more than five or six minutes, yet in that short space of time half the Italian battlefleet had been put out of action.

'About 20 seconds after I dropped my torpedo at the *Cavour* I ran into a lot of flak from a nearby destroyer and crashed in the harbour. I eventually surfaced and swam to a floating dock, hotly pursued by armour-piercing and incendiary bullets. I climbed on to the dock and was immediately set upon by about six Italians, and I feel I enjoy the doubtful distinction of being the first British naval officer to be captured by enemy dockyard workers. My observer and I became prisoners of war after that, first with the Italians and later in Germany.'

To give an overall view of this tremendous victory, included here are the views of some of the other survivors of the action — first from Lt-Cdr J. W. Neale DSC, RN (Retd), from the first wave, who at that time was a sub-lieutenant observer and was crewed with Sub-Lt Sparke of 815 Squadron:

'Our morale was very high and we had a wonderful briefing about Taranto. I reckon I knew more about the harbour at that time than the harbourmaster himself.

'We flew off in the dark at 170 miles range. My navigator's cockpit was full with an overload petrol tank so I sat in the air gunner's seat. It was so windy that we put our charts under sheets of Perspex on our chartboards and slid them under the Lewis gun.

'We all realised that this was one of those nights when we had more than the usual chance of being knocked down, and I — like most of the others — wore my best uniform. If you were going to be a prisoner of war, you might as well be properly dressed!

'Our form of attack was to stagger up to our ceiling of about 9,000ft and make the final approach throttled back to deceive the sound locators, diving very steeply in the last run-in to give us some

speed. We were all used by now to being shot at, but this barrage was quite fantastic — a complete ring of fire round the great harbour with all calibre weapons firing inwards over their fleet in a solid flat cone. My pilot flew magnificently. I remember passing him the course for home before we got too involved and he set this on his compass in case anything happened to me. We flew at an average height of 15ft — passing under most of the gunfire — marvelling all the time they could not hit us although the run across the target area was nearly two miles each way. I remember there was quite a lot of moon, and with the masses of tracer and with our own flares dropped by specially detailed aircraft it was very much lit up. We ran to within half a mile of the *Cavour* battleship, dropped our torpedo and spun round for the return. I remember timing the torpedo's run with my stopwatch. The little explosion I saw after 110 seconds was most disappointing, and it was not until afterwards we realised that the new magnetic pistol on the warhead was set to run too deeply to show much result. Sparke and I were the first ones back to the ship and I can remember great surprise when all the aircraft but one were eventually flying round and landing back on. I thought that we would have been the only ones to come away from that lot alive. Also, I can remember feeling thankful to the

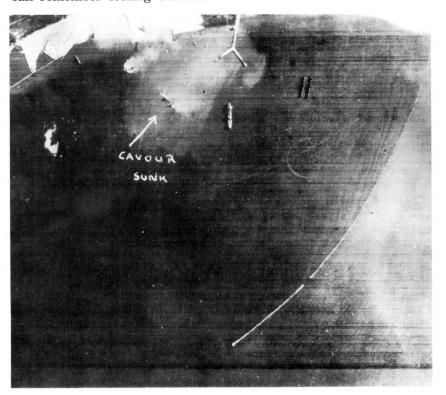

Italians for leaving the light on in one of their lighthouses on the heel of Italy — it helped my navigation considerably on the way home.'

The leader of the second strike, Lt-Cdr J. W. Hale, was more concerned with broader matters:

'My principal memories of the attack are the extra anxiety I felt as Squadron Commander because of the contaminated petrol in *Illustrious*. Three aircraft had been lost because of this during the previous two days and on the morning of 11 November the carburettors on all the aircraft were stripped down and cleaned and then refilled with petrol. The feeling was that someone else might go into the sea from the same cause. Apart from this, I felt much calmer than at other times when we had taken off for a night raid. I suppose this was because we all realised the terrific magnitude of the occasion, and this dwarfed the feeling of what might happen to me.

'I particularly remember the great cloud of flak that went up to greet Williamson when we were still about 70 miles away and my observer said "There's Taranto". This flak never stopped from then until we arrived about an hour later, and I thought at the time the Italians must be very worried and frightened. There were no searchlights, which surprised me because they would have blinded us. Apart from some fires ashore, there was nothing to indicate what damage had been done. It was wonderful to hear next day that three battleships had been hit and a few cruisers. I think the reason for the success was the great experience of all the aircrews. We were all peacetime trained and came from four squadrons undiluted even after a year of war and I believe that all the pilots had at least 800 hours' flying experience.'

Capt A. W. F. Sutton DSC, RN (Retd), a lieutenant at the time, was the observer for Lt F. M. A. Torrens-Spence:

'I was in the second striking force that night. We sighted the lighthouse on the tip of the heel of Italy, Santa Maria di Leucia, on the way in to the Gulf, fixed ourselves on it and then held off to the west. But we were detected — the enemy had very good sound detectors — and anti-aircraft guns hopefully opened fire as we passed along 15 miles offshore. When we were about 60 miles off Taranto we saw the place — a great

greenish-coloured cone of anti-aircraft fire, for the Italians were still keeping things going after the first attack had retired. We made to the northwest of the town, crossing the coast at around 9,000ft and then crossed and re-crossed the coastline to put off the anti-aircraft guns which had started to get uncomfortably accurate as we approached the harbour. The noise of the breaking waves on the beach tends to confuse the sound locators if you do that.

'The flare droppers had been detached as we crossed the coast and our leader, Lt-Cdr Hale, now ordered their release, with him starting his dive as they did so. At this moment the dive bombers should have run in to bomb the cruisers in the inner harbour to attract their fire, but we did not have enough aircraft in the ship to provide bombers for the second wave so there was nothing to draw the Italians' fire from us. As we went down they put up an intense box barrage for us to fly through. In a box barrage all the guns are fired in an imaginary box which is placed ahead of the aircraft. The rest of the sub-flight of three followed him down, and then over we went and down in that screaming torpedo dive . . . the Swordfish ahead of us had been hit, we saw an orange flash of flame and he spun away out of control. [This was the final moments of Swordfish 'E4H' flown by Bayly and Slaughter, the only casualties of the attack.] All the close-range weapons had opened fire. We could see multiple batteries by the entrance to the inner harbour pouring stuff out — right next to our dropping position. We pulled out a bit to starboard; tracer and incendiaries and a horrible thing we called "flaming onions" came streaming up at us. We came down a bit short, found ourselves down over the cruisers and pulled out — with that terrific jolt in the stomach as you pull out of a full torpedo dive — over the masts of the cruisers and down to our dropping height on the other side. The cruisers saw us and opened fire, we could see the tracers streaming along past us, seeming to float along. We found we had been in too close to one of the old "Cavour" battleships to attack her but now we were motoring in over the water towards one of their fine new "Littorios" . . . she saw us and opened fire — the flash of her close-range weapons stabbed at us as, first one, then another opened up along her entire length. We were coming in on her beam and were at the centre of an

incredible crossfire from the cruisers, battleships and shore batteries. No worries about clear range or gun zones for the Italians, they just fired everything they had, except the 15in ones. I could see the shots from the battleships bursting among the cruisers and merchant ships and the place stank of cordite and incendiaries with smoke everywhere. Torrens-Spence fired the torpedo — it did not come off — the magnetic release had failed! He finally managed to release at 700yd, by which time that "Littorio" battleship just about extended over the whole horizon, and we seemed to be looking down the muzzles of the close-range guns. A steep turn to starboard, straighten out, then "smack", we had hit the water, we're down, but we weren't, we hit with wheels only and Torrens-Spence pulled away through the balloon barrage flying between the floats and eventually out of that cauldron of fire. Suddenly everything was quiet. No one was firing at us. Relaxing, we set course for the gap between the forts out of the moonpath and got away really low down — so low in fact we did not see two defence ships in the harbour entrance. We sailed up over their masts as they opened up with just about every gun they had — to no avail, we were clear and on our way home.'

Most of the other crews who attacked Taranto that night told similar stories — Lt Charles Lamb said, 'As a flare dropper I had a bird's-eye view of the whole attack, and was amazed that anyone survived because of the flak from the harbour defences and the entire Italian fleet.'

Sub-Lt W. C. Sarra: 'When our sub-flight started climbing through thick cloud I lost the others. My observer and I were heading for Taranto alone. Very worrying, but a bit later I saw Lt-Cdr Williamson's formation lights and we rejoined the squadron. When we arrived at Taranto it seemed as though all hell had broken loose from the ground and I could not find my target. Eventually I noticed the seaplane base in the inner harbour and my observer, Jack Bowker, and I decided to bomb that instead. We were losing height all the time and when the bombs went off we wondered for a moment whether we had blown ourselves up. However, we got a hit and headed for home. Next morning we counted 17 holes in the aircraft from the anti-aircraft fire, including two from a bullet that had gone up between my legs!'

Sub-Lt J. Bowker, Sarra's observer, remembers:
'As we approached Grand Harbour the first shore guns winked, followed by air flashes and woofs through the Gosport tubes. Within seconds everything opened up — heavy anti-aircraft guns, pom-poms, machine guns, and, just as we released our bombs I clearly saw a gentleman standing by the slipway crane firing his rifle at us! We dropped our bomb load from 500ft and as we levelled out there was a tremendous roar as the hangar went up.'

The Italians' shore defences blasted off 13,389 rounds: 7,000 rounds by the 3in batteries, 1,750 by the 4in batteries and the remainder by pom-poms and other automatic weapons. No record was made of the number of rounds fired by the ships' crews, but no matter, the Italian battlefleet would not present a major threat to the Mediterranean war zone for some time to come.

When the results of the attack became known it was found that the six torpedo Swordfish from the first strike of 12 obtained two hits on *Littorio*, damaging her severely, and a hit on the *Conte Di Cavour*, which sank in shallow water. A third hit was probably made on the *Littorio* but the torpedo failed to go off. The second strike also made a hit on *Littorio* and the *Caio Duilio*. The bombing aircraft wrecked the seaplane base, which had provided the aircraft that shadowed the British fleet. Hits were also made on other warships, and oil storage tanks were set on fire: two 250lb bombs hit the cruiser *Trento* and a destroyer but failed to explode. The *Cavour* sank, and although she was raised later, she was not back in service by the end of the war. *Littorio* did not return to full service for more than six months, and the *Caio Duilio* had to be beached in a sinking state, her repairs taking eight months. What the final results could have been is anybody's guess, for another strike by 12 Swordfish from the *Illustrious* was planned for the following night, but it had to be cancelled because of bad weather.

When the news of the raid leaked out the whole world was thrilled, and none more so than the British nation. Capt Boyd of the *Illustrious* remarked:
'It is impossible to praise too highly those who in these comparatively slow machines made studied and accurate attacks in the midst of intense anti-aircraft fire. It is hoped that this victory will be considered a suitable reward to those whose work and faith in the Fleet Air Arm has made it possible.'

Winston Churchill addressed the House of Commons on 13 November 1940:
'The result affects decisively the balance of naval power in the Mediterranean, and also carries with it reactions upon the naval situation in every quarter of the globe. I feel sure the House will regard these results as highly satisfactory and as reflecting the greatest credit upon the Admiralty and upon Admiral Cunningham, the Commander-in-Chief in the Mediterranean, and above all on our pilots of the Fleet Air Arm . . .'

After the congratulations and acknowledgement came the decorations — but it was a bitter disappointment to those taking part when the awards came through. The squadron commanders each received the DSO, their observers the DSC, and Capt Patch and Lt Goodwin also received the DSC — and that was it. The ship's company was shocked, and angry. Many felt the leaders deserved a Victoria Cross for attacking such a heavily defended target in slow and outdated biplanes. The New Year Honours List of 1941 announced the CB for Adm Lyster, and the CBE for Capt Boyd and Capt Bridge of the *Eagle*. Six months later the rest of the gallant crews received their recognition as new awards were announced — but by then it was too late, for one-third of those taking part in the Taranto raid were dead, killed in action, many of them in the subsequent bombing of *Illustrious*. But the bitter pill was that there was no recognition for those aboard *Illustrious* who had worked so hard and strived to get the maximum effort both from themselves and their aircraft.

Right:
The *Littorio* with decks awash and supporting ships alongside. *Italian Navy*

Aircraft and Crews in the Attack on Taranto

FIRST WAVE

Aircraft	Pilot/Observer	Warload	Decoration
L4A	Lt-Cdr K. Williamson Lt N. Scarlett-Streatfield	Torpedo	DSO DSC
L4C	Sub-Lt P. Sparke DSC Sub-Lt J. Neale	Torpedo	Bar to DSC DSC
L4K	Lt N. Kemp Sub-Lt R. A. Bailey	Torpedo	DSC DSC
L4M	Lt I. H. Swayne Sub-Lt J. Buscall RNVR	Torpedo	MID MID
L4R	Sub-Lt A. S. D. Macauley Sub-Lt A. L. O. Wray	Torpedo	DSC DSC
E4F	Lt M. R. Maund Sub-Lt W. Bull	Torpedo	MID MID
L4P	Lt L. J. Kiggell Lt H. R. B. Janvrin	Flares & bombs	DSC DSC
L5B	Lt C. Lamb Lt K. Grieve	Flares & bombs	MID MID
L4L	Sub-Lt W. C. Sarra Sub-Lt J. Bowker	Bombs	MID MID
E5A	Capt O. Patch RM Lt D. Goodwin	Bombs	DSC DSC
L4H	Sub-Lt A. Forde Sub-Lt A. Mardel-Ferreira	Bombs	MID MID
E5Q	Lt J. Murray Sub-Lt S. Paine	Bombs	MID MID

SECOND WAVE

Aircraft	Pilot/Observer	Warload	Decoration
L5A	Lt-Cdr J. W. Hale Lt G. A. Carline	Torpedo	DSO DSC
L5H	Lt C. S. C. Lea Sub-Lt P. D. Jones	Torpedo	DSC DSC
L5K	Lt F. M. A. Torrens-Spence Lt A. W. F. Sutton	Torpedo	DSC DSC
E4H	Lt G. W. Bayly Lt J. H. Slaughter	Torpedo	MID MID
E5H	Lt T. W. G. Wellham Lt P. Humphreys	Torpedo	MID MID
L5B	Lt R. W. V. Hamilton Sub-Lt J. R. Weekes	Flares & bombs	DSC DSC
L4F	Lt R. Skelton Sub-Lt E. Perkins RNVR	Flares & bombs	MID MID
L5F	Lt E. W. Clifford Lt G. R. M. Going	Flares & bombs	DSC DSC
L5Q	Lt S. Morford Sub-Lt R. Green	Bombs	MID MID

MID = Mentioned in despatches

Postscript

As mentioned previously, many of those aircrew on the Taranto raid were subsequently killed aboard *Illustrious*, almost exactly two months later.

Early in the New Year of 1941, *Illustrious*, with the battleships *Warspite* and *Valiant*, had left Alexandria to meet and escort a convoy for Malta and Greece, taking over from Force H at a changeover point west of Malta. On 10 January the Mediterranean Fleet had taken over the convoy; it was a brilliant blue-sky day and shortly after 10.00hrs *Illustrious* flew off five Fulmars for CAP (Combat Air Patrol) duties. Soon after 11.00hrs, Italian aircraft appeared, but the Fulmars shot two down and drove the rest off — but not for long, because at 12.20 Italian torpedo bombers made an attack low down from the south. The rest of the Fulmars, being refuelled and armed, were quickly ranged and flown off. However, it was too late, and the first bomb hit *Illustrious* at 12.38 — and it wasn't an Italian one, it was from German Ju87 Stukas. It was a superb attack. There were apparently two formations of enemy aircraft, one of about 30 concentrating on the *Illustrious*, and the other on *Warspite* and *Valiant*. Divided into three sub-flights, the Stukas, changing height and speed to fox the gun predictors, came in from different directions, diving from 12,000ft to around 800ft before releasing their bombs and then spraying the ship with machine gun fire as they passed over. Within seven minutes it was over... Air Fitter Whitley was there:

'The bar was still open and I estimated I had time for a drink before "carry on" sounded. I was just taking the glass when all hell was let loose, the for'd 4.5s were each side of the bar and something blasted the glass right out of my hand. I set off for my action station which was in the hangar. This involved passing through the port paravane lobby and when I got to the ladder leading to it there were bomb splashes all alongside the ship, seemingly in large numbers and closer than before so I decided that I would be better off if I kept a bit of ship between myself and the nasties. All the ship's guns were in action and above the crack of the heavies and the rattle of the pom-poms I heard an aircraft pulling out of its dive. I had never heard a Stuka before, but I knew what it was alright. My first reaction when the ship was hit was disbelief, it felt as if it had been picked up and dropped back in the water. After a repeat, and another, I was convinced that our swan around the Med was over and that it was an entirely different war with the Luftwaffe on the other side. I could now see that the ship was steaming at high speed, round in circles with smoke pouring out aft and in sight of the Italian fortress at Pantellaria. At that time it didn't seem to be a very good place to be, especially as I moved toward the hangar and found we were on fire at both ends. The sight that met my eyes in the hangar did little to improve my confidence. The armoured doors were almost closed and through them, silhouetted against a wall of flame, were battered Swordfish, spares

Right:
A fine view of HMS *Illustrious* showing the 620ft flightdeck with a Swordfish being ranged to fly. It was from *Illustrious* that the famous raid on Taranto was launched on 11 November 1940. The *Illustrious* was one of four new carriers ordered in 1937/38, the other three being the *Victorious*, *Formidable* and *Indomitable*. Her aircraft complement changed from 33 early in the war to 54 by 1945 when her flightdeck had been lengthened to 740ft.

from the deckhead, shredded fire-screens and, a row of torpedoes — which I knew were primed ready for use! I jumped into the lobby, pulled the lever that shut off the hangar ventilation, pulled the chain to start the spray pumps and opened the wheel to turn on the sprays. Moving up on the flight deck I found the for'd lift was bent like the roof of a house, the aft lift on its end in the well, a hole in the flight deck on the centre line and clouds of smoke every-where. I helped run a hose from the for'd end to the hole in the deck but only a trickle came from it and the deck was becoming so hot it was burning my shoes. The crews from the for'd 4.5s were yelling for ammunition while the after turrets were badly damaged but had ammo — so we started carrying them along the flight deck — some nearly as tall as me. The second wave of enemy bombers appeared and the tannoy started up again but there was no damage this time. Eventually all non-essential personnel were told to get below decks so we found a space to rest in and sat eating bully beef sandwiches — when suddenly a hatch opened and a dirty face appeared to ask "What's been happening?". It was one of the stokers; they worked in incredible temperatures of up to 140 deg to save the ship. The hangar was still ablaze with flames shooting 50ft up the aft lift well and firefighting efforts having little effect. A further raid just after four o'clock was beaten off but one hit was made again near the aft lift — 30 of the ship's company died instantly. Throughout the evening battered and exhausted men continued the battle to contain the fires and at 10.15 to everyone's relief *Illustrious* tied up at Parlatorio Wharf in Grand Harbour, Malta. A fleet of ambulances took away the wounded. The next day we started to clear up the mess. The hangar, dimly lit by emergency light-ing, was a shambles, burnt-out Fulmars and damaged Swordfish everywhere. The stench of cordite burning, and the sickly smell of burned and mutilated bodies will never be forgotten. The Luftwaffe came over again and again to try and sink the *Illustrious* but they never managed it. When she was ready to sail for Alexandria, and then on to the USA for repairs, I was told, "Sorry Whitley, we are putting you ashore in Malta for a rest". The rest turned out to be two years with 830 Squadron during the siege . . .'

The casualties aboard *Illustrious* were 83 officers and men killed, 60 seriously wounded and 40 slightly wounded. Among the Taranto crews killed were Kemp, Skelton, Perkins, Clifford, Wray and Mardel-Ferreira. Going lost a leg and Morford was so badly burned that he required plastic surgery. Of those that survived, 11 others later lost their lives: Sparke transferred to fighters and collided with a German aircraft, Macauley crashed into the sea when the wings of his Swordfish folded up in a vertical power dive, Maund was killed on ops from Malta, and Hamilton and Weekes were shot down in an attack on Leros.

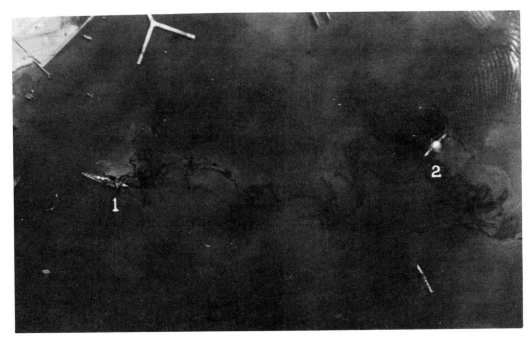

Left:
Another view of Taranto harbour the morning after the attack. Oil slicks can be seen leaking from the damaged ships.
IWM (CN1162)

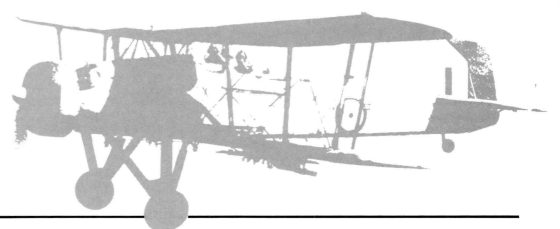

THE NIGHT I LAID
MY OWN FLAREPATH

On 27 March 1941 a Sunderland operating from the island of Malta sighted the Italian fleet heading towards Crete. The Mediterranean Fleet, which included *Formidable*, left Alexandria to intercept the convoy — and the action that became known as the Battle of Cape Matapan took place the next day. This action is recorded elsewhere, but it is not generally known that a Swordfish floatplane was used to observe and report the positions of the two fleets. The observer in the aircraft that day was Lt-Cdr A. S. Bolt, later Rear-Adm Bolt CB, DSO, DSC, who recorded his impression of the first sortie:

'I see from my flying log that we were catapulted from *Warspite* in Swordfish floatplane K8863, named *Lorna*, at 12.15hrs, and the flight actually lasted four hours forty minutes. The main forces were meeting at high speed. The battlefleet steaming to support the cruiser squadron at 23kt was expected to make contact with the advancing units of the Italian fleet within two hours at the most, when *Warspite* launched our aircraft for action/observation. My duties (as observer) were to obtain a visual link between the fleets as soon as possible and then to report generally on the tactical situation as seen from the air.

'During my briefing before take-off no instructions had been given to me about recovery at sea at the end of the patrol or about going to Suda Bay. I assumed that I would be given orders in the air according to the wishes of the Commander-in-Chief in the light of the tactical situation at the time. In *Warspite*, the Flag Captain assumed that the necessary orders for the aircraft's return to base would be given by the Chief of Staff . . . Hmmmm.

'The fleets did not make contact as expected, the Italian main force showing an inclination to press on to the southeast after the Fleet Air Arm torpedo attack. The safe endurance of my aircraft was about four and three-quarter hours, though we had on occasion achieved five hours under favourable conditions. My routine reports of fuel state evoked no response from *Warspite* until I reported only 15 minutes of fuel remaining. Suda Bay was over one hour's flying away, so a decision had to be made to recover or destroy the aircraft. In the event, the Commander-in-Chief decided to recover the aircraft although the fleet was in hot pursuit of the *Vittorio Veneto*, having been slowed, as we thought, by a torpedo hit from an aircraft from *Formidable*. My aircraft was ordered to alight ahead of the *Warspite*. With the crane swung out on the starboard side, the plan was to hook on as the ship steamed up to overtake the aircraft taxying on a parallel course. The sea was calm and my pilot, PO Rice, made a good landing about two cables ahead of the ship, turning on to a parallel course and taxied at about 10kt with the ship coming up fast astern. We had never practised this method of recovery and were a good deal disturbed by the bow wave. PO Rice turned the aircraft to starboard as the bow wave came up and hit our floats square on the stern. I was then able to talk PO Rice to a position under the Thomas grab hook and PO Pacey, the TAG, hooked on first time at 16.55hrs. Lt-Cdr Copeman [later 4th Sea Lord] with whom we had had a good understanding on the recovery operation, hoisted us quickly clear of the water as soon as PO Pacey gave the hooked-on signal. The Swordfish was put on the catapult and refuelled while I went to make my peace on the Admiral's bridge. The *Warspite* only lost one mile through the water during the recovery and I do not believe she was doing less than 18kt at any moment during the operation.'

Petty Officer F. C. Rice DSM was the pilot of the Swordfish and he continues the story about the rest of that day:
'During the sortie the aircraft was carrying four 250lb armour-piercing and eight 40lb anti-personnel bombs. Lt-Cdr Bolt suggested that before we landed on the sea to be hoisted aboard *Warspite* that we jettison them. I flew to a position astern of the fleet and did this. On hitting the sea all the bombs went off. I forget what was said between us on the Gosport tube but the remark from him was:

"The bombs exploded!"
"I know, I dropped them live"
"Why?"
"Because I wanted to see if they worked."

'I can't print his reply. The explosions caused a little consternation in the destroyer screen as they thought we had spotted a submarine, and I think it was *Hotspur* that rushed over to investigate. PO Pacey, my TAG, informed her what had happened with the Aldis lamp. After that we landed on the sea and hoisted aboard Warspite.

'We were catapulted again at 17.45hrs in the same aircraft, putting four flare floats on the port light series rack as there was a possibility that we would have to alight at night on the open sea with no organised flare path. The task given us by the Staff Officer [Cdr A. J. Power] was to clear up the situation caused by conflicting reports about the position, course, speed, composition and disposition of the enemy fleet. It was known that the *Vittorio Veneto's* speed had been reduced, but it was not clear whether another force reported consisted of battleships or 8in gun cruisers. We carried out our reconnaissance duties and passed out reports by W/T (in morse of course) direct to Alexandria W/T station at a distance of some 400 miles. We had carried out a great deal of practice with this station during dawn and dusk anti-submarine patrols from Alexandria and it was very satisfying that PO Pacey was able to clear some dozen Operational Immediate messages

Left:
It was in a Swordfish floatplane such as this that PO Rice spotted for the Battle of Cape Matapan and afterwards landed in the light of a flarepath on the sea.

in a matter of minutes. These signals, repeated by Alexandria W/T to Malta and Gibraltar, were received immediately in Whitehall W/T and the Admiralty had them nearly as soon as the Commander-in-Chief in *Warspite*. As an airborne W/T operator my TAG, Maurice Pacey, deserved great credit. I also learned later, reading Admiral Iachino's report from *Vittorio Veneto*, that he picked up all our signals and it is gratifying to note from his report that we were only one knot out in estimating his speed.

'At sunset we saw the dusk torpedo attack by 826 and 829 Squadrons, plus two Swordfish from Crete. The Italian fleet had formed itself into a compact mass which made it a very difficult target. I saw the attack develop from a position about five miles astern of the Italian fleet and regretted very much that we had jettisoned our bombs earlier. The attack was most spectacular, the Italians pouring out vast quantities of coloured tracer from their close-range weapons. At 19.50hrs we were relieved by an Albacore from *Formidable* and we took departure for Suda Bay at 2,000ft.

'After about half an hour I inquired when we might expect a landfall, and where, as it was getting rather dark.

"21.13hrs Akra Spatha, 1,214ft"
"Where is Akra Spatha, sir?"
"It is the northwest tip of Crete."

'At about five past nine I observed a large black mass ahead to starboard which I reported to the observer. He informed me that it was the mountain range on the northwest tip of Crete. At 21.13hrs we passed over Akra Spatha. I then suggested to Lt-Cdr Bolt that we ask Maleme, which was about 10 miles south of our position, if we could land on the grass airfield there. He then told me we might damage the floats doing this! An understatement on his part, I thought. Lt-Cdr Bolt then suggested that, as we had flare floats, we should go and alight on Suda Bay, the landing path being lit with our own flares. I had landed and taken off from there a couple of times in daylight so I knew the harbour. We set course for Akra Malchas lighthouse (negative light) and on arriving overhead turned south for Suda Bay. Lt-Cdr Bolt gave me a wind of 250°/10kts. I then turned into the bay on this heading at 1,000ft and dropped the flares from the Mickey Mouse (I forget

the correct name for the flare-dropping distributor) at 100yd intervals outside the boom. Reports from the back seat:

"Flares gone, first one burning brightly"
"Don't muck about, they only burn for five minutes — high ground to port 2,000ft"

'Steep turn to port on to 070°, all flares burning, turn again to port about one mile from first flare, losing height. Flare path right ahead. Better than Air Traffic put out and much quicker. Line up, continue descent and sit on water by number two flare — time, 21.25hrs. After about two minutes all the flares went out and it was very dark!

"What do we do now?" (from me)
"We are now waterborne, steer 310° for the boom gate."

'Pacey climbed up on to the centre section and used the Aldis lamp as a headlight as we taxied at about 20kt on this heading for about five miles, which seemed to take a very long time. Also, every time I throttled back the Aldis went dim as our battery was getting low! At about 22.00hrs we identified ourselves to the patrol vessel on the boom. He enquired —

"What type of vessel?"
"Floatplane."

'His amazement was illustrated by the switching on of an enormous searchlight which confirmed our statement. God knows what he must have thought. He opened up the boom gate and we taxied into the harbour. A motor boat from the *York* guided us to a mooring for the night and then ferried us to the *Carlisle*. Total time airborne for the day — 8 hours 20 minutes, of which two were at night with the only instruments being a P10 compass, a primitive turn-and-bank indicator and an even older type of altimeter fitted with only one needle which gave about one inch of movement for every thousand feet. As there was a shortage of spare instruments, we had surrendered our instrument panel to the carrier squadrons some time before.

'For our part in this operation the observer was awarded a bar to his DSC and the pilot and TAG were Mentioned in Despatches'.

STRINGBAGS FROM MALTA

When, after months of continuous operations from the island of Malta, No 830 Squadron virtually ceased to exist, one of its members sat down and wrote:

Empty Stringbag on the Safi strip
Why don't you fly tonight?
Is there shrapnel in your mainplanes,
Are your pistons slightly teased,
Have you got a bombhole in your pen?

Empty Stringbag on the Safi strip,
Why don't you fly tonight?
Did the riggers all forsake you,
Have they hidden underground,
Are they waiting for a hundred plus?

Empty tanks bunged up with rust,
Why don't you leak tonight?
Lousy brakes, smothered in dust,
Why don't you squeak tonight?

Empty Stringbag on the Safi strip,
My tears would be dry tonight,
If you'd only totter skywards,
With your Peggy grinding hard,
Empty Stringbag on the Safi strip.

They are poignant words, having great meaning to the brave crews who flew Swordfish from the bomb-battered island to take the war back to the enemy, to be a thorn in its side, and who flew again and again against the odds, and then flew yet again. Full details of the exploits of 830 Squadron (and other naval squadrons) are given in Kenneth Poolman's excellent book *Night Strike from Malta*. It is not my intention to try and emulate Mr Poolman but to present a few vignettes by people who were there; after all, it would be an injustice to the crews who flew from Malta to be excluded from a book about the Swordfish — without them there would be no story.

Malta itself was a small dusty island which was unfortunate enough to be located in a strategic position between Sicily and Libya, and thus held the key to the control of supply routes through and across the Mediterranean and along the North African coastline. The civil and military people on the island took everything the Axis forces threw at them, from trying to bomb them to the point of surrender, or trying to sink the vital supply ships bringing much-needed materials. The subsequent courage and stamina resulted in a much deserved George Cross — MALTA GC.

The origins of 830 Squadron go back to a training squadron which, to take advantage of the good weather in the Med, moved into Southern France and used the old deck landing training carrier *Argus* to complete such training for the pilots. Lt-Cdr Charles Wines, then a Petty Officer, was one such pilot:
'I arrived at Hyeres (Bas Aero Navale) near Toulon at the end of May 1940 with other Petty Officer pilots to complete our

Right:
The wreckage of an 830 Squadron Swordfish in its blast pen on Malta. Blast pens usually afforded protection to anything other than a direct hit — or flying shrapnel.
Lt-Cdr R. E. F. Kerrison

Below and far right:
These two views also depict the end of three Swordfish of 830 Squadron. Despite moving the aircraft around, the intensity of enemy air attacks was such that attrition rates later meant that the squadron rarely had two or three aircraft available, and Albacores supplemented and eventually took over most of the operational flying.
Lt-Cdr R. E. F. Kerrison; N. Gold

deck landing training on *Argus's* flight deck, the Squadron being 767. The French were at that time just about to collapse and the carrier left the area before we could land on her. We bombed Genoa on 6 June 1940, taking the Italians completely by surprise with no losses. On 18 June we left Hyeres for Bone in Algeria and there it was decided to send 12 Swordfish to Malta as 830 Squadron with Lt-Cdr F. D. Howie as CO. Petty Officer Freddie Parr and myself were the only rating pilots selected to stay. We arrived at Hal Far to find the airfield covered with buses and training aircraft as an anti-invasion device. We landed among them with no trouble much to the chagrin of the Wing Commander in charge, who considered

his plan foolproof. During the next few months we operated against the Italians in Sicily and Tripoli with bombs, mines and torpedoes.

The following incidents stick out in my memory:

16 October 1940 — My crew were Lt (O) Wanford and Naval Airman Pickles. When on a recce we came across a Cant 105 flying boat and engaged it in a dogfight. The Italian pilot must have thought he had a Gladiator to contend with. I got away most of my front gun ammo before the gun jammed and Pickles swore at me for not giving him sufficient opportunity to use his Lewis gun. The Cant got away at about 135kt to our 115. He could have been unarmed as we weren't hit.

'21 December 1940 — The only luck that really came my way to aid the war effort was when with Corporal Parker (later to be known as "Sailor" Parker, the Mosquito hero of European Mosquito raid fame) as my air gunner we were ordered to bomb the seaplane hangars and slipway at Tripoli. Whilst the AA fireworks (the Italians excelled in this type of defence) were engaging the rest of the squadron aircraft, I glided in with engine throttled back from the desert side and spread three 500lb HE and two sticks of incendiary bombs across the hangar clearly seen in the moonlight. According to Parker the results were

something worth seeing. I was too busy making myself small in my cockpit whilst diving down to sea level, "balls out" with everything that the defences had turned on us as soon as they heard my engine open up. Years later, whilst serving with a Malta-based Mosquito communications squadron, I got an opportunity to walk over my old target area and actually spoke to the night watchman who had been on duty during the attack. He said that nine assorted seaplanes and flying boats had gone up as well as MTBs and patrol craft which were up the slipway for repair.

'10 January 1941 — 830 Squadron had been ordered to attack cruisers and destroyers which had been photographed sheltering in Palermo harbour, Sicily. We set off in four flights of three aircraft and over Sicily I got separated from my flight in cloud and made my way to Palermo by flying west to the coast then round the coast to Palermo. Over the target Parker and I saw a single Swordfish dive steeply at a merchant ship in the dry dock and its bombs explode between the ship and dry dock walls, which could not have done it much good. On landing at Hal Far hours afterwards we were surprised to learn that the other aircraft we had seen over the target was piloted by Freddie Parr and that the other 10 Swordfish had returned after presumably being

ordered back because they were unable to get through the weather. There must have been a few red faces in the wardroom that night!

'Both Freddie Parr and myself were trained at Kalfrana to drop torpedoes even though rating pilots were not supposed to. I polished and cosseted my only torpedo and was shot down after my one and only torpedo attack against a tanker in a convoy off the Tunisian coast. Due to the escorts' fire I had to fly up to, and over my target with the predictable result of being filled full of holes and lucky enough to be able to crash on the beach at Hammamet partially blinded by oil from a fractured oil tank. I was to spend nearly two years as a PoW in Tunis, Medea and Laghouat before being released in late 1942 when the Allies landed in Algiers.'

What was it like for the groundcrews? Fred Whitley remembers only too well:
'I shared an aircraft with a LAM(E) Nicholson and it was a change to have just one aircraft to look after. We really worked on that Swordfish, stripping out unnecessary bits and pieces, setting up the rigging wires carefully, and it had an outstanding performance — but it was a waste of time, the others couldn't keep up with it! We also changed the starter if it failed to start the engine first go, and oddly enough on one occasion, we moved the aircraft to Luqa (a scheme

so that if one airfield was bombed we would have some aircraft left) and it would not start — just as well, as the airfield was strafed by 109s just as we would have been airborne. About this time we got our hands on an ASV and really thought ourselves something when it was fitted — it was destroyed shortly after by the accidental release of a flare on the ground at Hal Far! Keeping the aircraft serviceable was a struggle, they were kept in pens which protected them against all but a direct hit or falling shrapnel. When the built-in system became u/s, filling aircraft from four-gallon cans was a long miserable task. Food became scarce and it was remarkable that we were able to keep operating. Hal Far was gradually destroyed and we lived in surrounding villages or at Kalafrana. We led a nomadic existence; when we had lost all our aircraft we were loaned out to RAF squadrons and also helped out when new deliveries of fighters arrived. We had to carry a card which was punched for each meal — which meant that we couldn't go round for "seconds". I was flown out of Malta in October 1942 which ended my three years' involvement with the dear old Stringbag.'

Nat Gold was a TAG with 830 Squadron and he recalls some aspects of his one and only anti-submarine patrol:
'In the early hours of Thursday 24 July 1941, two Swordfish took-off from Malta to search for and provide anti-submarine patrols for a very important convoy on its way in from Gibraltar.

These two were unable to find the convoy and two others were sent off. I was in one with Lt Bibby as we took off in the darkness. As daylight arrived I felt more comfortable because I could see everything, but a little apprehensive as we were now vulnerable to attacks by marauding 109s. We settled down and it wasn't long before we spotted some ships, some were obviously already damaged and lay low in the water. I signalled the cruiser with my Aldis lamp and that formality over I sent off a coded message to Malta to say we were in contact. I then casually looked up and to my horror a whole squadron of Stukas were just astern of us. I grabbed the Gosport tube and yelled to my pilot, "Stukas astern". He banked slightly to see for himself, "How many?" he asked, "I've counted 12 so far" I replied. "Any fighters?", "I can't see any, but they might be up sun". "Right, let's get out of here", and with that we dived down to wave-top level and zoomed all over the place in case we were attacked. I managed to cling on and remain standing — gun at the ready — but we were in the clear and I was able to watch the Stukas carry out their attack, not with any success I am glad to say. When the attack was over we proceeded on course, wondering if there were to be more attacks as we approached Malta. The convoy was fairly spread out and as we moved from one area to another we noticed something on the water — glory be, it was the other Swordfish, which for some reason had run out of petrol. The Swordfish was floating nicely and crew

of three were just stepping out into their dinghy. We made several diving approaches over them and dropped a smoke float. We then flew across to the convoy consisting of five merchant ships and five destroyers and signalled the leading destroyer: "Swordfish in sea, can you pick up the crew?" They said they would and then for the next few hours I was extremely busy sending and receiving radio messages to and fro from Malta as we had to take on the other Swordfish's role and patrol both parts of the convoy. On one of our trips back and forth we spotted something else in the water and went down to have a look — it turned out to be a floating mine. Lt Bibby asked me to have a go at it with the Lewis gun and manoeuvred into position. I let fly — it was great fun and helped relieve the monotony of the patrol. I could see my tracers pinging off the mine but it didn't explode, even though I wasted a pan of ammunition on it. We dropped a smoke float to mark it and then signalled the leading destroyer — "Floating mine on your port beam, can you deal with it?" They replied that they could and we carried on patrolling. As we neared Malta we got more and more concerned about air attacks but to our great surprise none materialised — but the next day Jerry made up for it by several bombing raids on Grand Harbour causing lots of damage — even the Italians bombed from high level which was unusual for them.'

One of the torpedo pilots with 830 Squadron was Lt-Cdr Roger Kerrison who, as a young sub-lieutenant, carried out 23 night torpedo strikes, as well as daylight bombing and anti-submarine patrols. Although not normally accident-prone he went through rather a traumatic series of events while involved with Swordfish. In June 1941 he was injured when the MV *Georgic* was bombed at Port Tewfic, also losing his first logbook and spending four weeks in hospital with burns. In August 1941 he was piloting a Swordfish that hit a Martlet on a night take-off, caught fire and later crashed. Then in September he was being ferried to Malta in a Sunderland when it made a poor landing and sank, taking his second logbook! A few days later, while out on a night familiarisation flight, his aircraft's engine cut and he had to ditch, before being picked up by an air-sea rescue launch. The following month he was carrying out a dive-bombing attack

on Lampadusa harbour when a shell exploded in the fuselage, the Swordfish being a complete write-off. Next, in March 1942 his cabin on Malta was bombed and he lost his third logbook. After Malta he flew Avengers with 832 Squadron, and later commanded 756 Squadron at Katakurunda, Ceylon.

Returning to Malta, Roger Kerrison recalls one of his night torpedo attacks: 'Flying long hours at night over the sea in a single-engined aircraft, sometimes in bad weather, was a drain on the nerves — wondering if fuel would last out, if the engine would keep turning and, if we would ever find the island again. Flak of course was very frightening in an open cockpit. One could see it coming in clouds, hear it sizzling and cracking past, and, worst of all, you could smell it! When I joined 830 Squadron in the middle of September 1941 it was already an elite and very experienced squadron. Some pilots had already done a considerable number of operations from Malta, and all had joined from other squadrons, having taken part in such operations as Matapan, Taranto and *Bismarck*. I was very much the new boy straight from school, and, because of a shortage of observers, only had a TAG in the back seat for my first two or three operations. Then Lt "Steve" Stevenson RN joined the squadron and teamed up with me as my observer, doing some 25 operational flights together. I remember one such trip on the night of 22/23 November 1941. Four Swordfish were involved, one three-seat aircraft carrying an

overload fuel tank under the fuselage, this was the flare machine and was to be flown by the leader of the strike, Lt Bill Garthwaite DSC, RNVR, with Sub-Lt Tony Gillingham RNVR working the ASV set. The other three aircraft were two-seaters as they carried the overload tank in the rear cockpit. These were flown by Lt O'Brien RN, Sub-Lt Roger Kerrison RNVR, and Sub-Lt Wheeler RNVR. We had a preliminary briefing to the effect that an important convoy consisting of merchant ships escorted by three cruisers and 12 destroyers had been seen off Sicily and probably making for Benghazi. An ASV Wellington, with an 830 Squadron observer to navigate, would try to find the convoy

after dark and report its position, course and speed.

'This came through at about 10pm and after a final briefing we taxied the Swordfish to the end of the flare-path with an erk on either wing-tip to avoid dropping into recent bomb craters. The flare-path was just three dim lights switched on for the few seconds needed for take-off or landing. The strike aircraft switched on their navigation lights to form up over a flame float about 12 miles from the island, then switched them off to formate on dim blue formation lights. It was a black night of strong winds, nine-tenths cloud and occasional heavy rain squalls. It was during one of these squalls that Wheeler lost formation in the dark and returned to Malta with his torpedo. Every so often an observer would chuck out a flame-float to check wind drift.

'After some two and half hours, the convoy was picked up on ASV at a range of about 20 miles so we closed. When the ASV indicated that the strike was over

the target at about 5,000ft the leader gave the signal to break, the torpedo aircraft breaking one way and the flare aircraft the other. The leader then dropped about six flares and luckily we were in the right place to see a large number of ships below. I immediately started a diving attack on a merchantman. Suddenly, Steve, my observer, pointed and shouted that there was a bigger ship over there and I switched my attack to it, which we saw to be one of the cruisers. We were seen as we crossed the destroyer screen at about 100ft and flak started coming up at as from several directions, including clouds of it from our target. We got down to 50ft and dropped our torpedo at 500yd, holding the aircraft straight and level for three seconds for our torpedo to drop properly and hoping I had correctly guessed the target's speed. We then got right down to the deck under the flak, escaping under the target's stern and up into the darkness — and as we did so Steve opened up with his Lewis gun, giving away our position and frightening me out of my wits! As we climbed away we could see the bubbles of our running torpedo meet the cruiser, which was turning under full rudder to avoid it. There was a high column of water under X turret as our magnetic head exploded under the ship's bottom. The cruiser made a complete circle and stopped in a cloud of smoke. All this was also seen and confirmed by the leader circling overhead. Flak continued to fly in all directions, some bouncing off an unlucky destroyer. It then concentrated low over the water as Lt O'Brien made his attack. Unfortunately he was shot down before he could drop and he and his observer, Griffiths, were lost. After watching for a few more minutes we started on the long journey back to Malta. In due course we saw the welcoming cone of searchlights over the island, crept in along the coast and plopped down on the dimly lit flare-path. We were met by two erks with torches who guided us back to our blast-pen and I shut down. We had been in the air for slightly over six hours.

'It later transpired that our cruiser was the 9,988-ton *Duca Degli Abruzzi* which needed eight months for repairs. The British submarine *Utmost*, patrolling nearby, saw the flak, crept in and torpedoed the heavy cruiser *Trieste*, which sank. The convoy turned back to Sicily, thus depriving Rommel of badly needed supplies. As I said, I did 25

Top:
The damage to Sub-Lt Coxon's port mainplanes after an attack by Bf109s.
Cdr C. R. Coxon

Above:
A view showing the cannon damage to V4587 after a pass by attacking Bf109s. Only quick action on the part of Sub-Lt Coxon saved the crew from being killed as the second burst would have entered the cockpit.
Cdr C. R. Coxon

operations with Steve before he volunteered one night to fly with Sub-Lt Maurice Swithinbank whose observer was sick. They were last seen on fire over the convoy, probably knocked down by a Ju88 night-fighter which sometimes escorted convoys.'

But it wasn't only the convoys that Malta found a problem: returning aircraft had to be aware of enemy aircraft over the island day or night — and then again, it wasn't always the enemy that was the danger. Cdr Cedric Coxon has cause to recall one such day:

'The squadron [830] needed replacement aircraft and the plan was to send one pilot, Acting Sub-Lt (A) C. R. J. Coxon RN, one observer, Acting Sub-Lt (A) Davies RNVR, and one TAG, to Fayid to collect two new Swordfish plus a replacement pilot. We duly took passage to Alexandria (together with some Luftwaffe aircrew prisoners) in the MV *Breconshire*, which, after returning to Malta, was sunk in Kalafrana Bay by Ju88s. We survived one Ju88 attack on the way to Alexandria. Finally, after several days clearing problems, we set off from Dekheila in V4587 and worked our way along the coast to Benghazi, the "stepping-off" place. The aircraft were fitted with long-range tanks on the torpedo rack and our baggage put where the TAG usually sat. The late afternoon was fine and clear as we neared Malta and our W/T message with ETA was accepted and we were given clearance to enter Malta airspace. An air-raid alert a few minutes later was not given to us, so we dived to "beat-up" the officers' mess in traditional style. Meanwhile Hurricanes were scrambled as the German air-raid was located. The Army, apparently having no knowledge of our approach, thought the long-range tanks were bombs and opened fire on us! Now usually, when firing at Ju88s they missed astern, but with our much slower speed they were missing ahead, but not by much! The other Swordfish was on my right and the Bofors' red tracer was cutting across my bow from the left. As if this was not enough my observer suddenly yelled over the Gosport tube and at that instant the first burst of red cannon tracer from a 109 passed down my starboard side between the two aircraft. I quickly commenced a side-slip to starboard, waving away the other Swordfish. This saved me from the next burst which hit the port wings and as I pulled into a

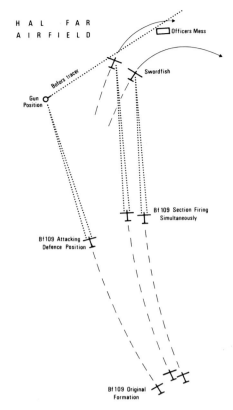

steep turn the last burst hit the tailplane. The three 109s that made the one pass were reputed to have been shot down by the defenders but I have no confirmation of this. We landed and parked — the other Swordfish being destroyed a few minutes later by a Ju88 bombing raid.'

It is perhaps fitting to end this section with the words of AVM H. P. Lloyd MC, DFC, ADC, who was Air Officer Commanding, RAF Mediterranean, at that time and was reported in *The Times of Malta* for 18 December 1941:

'At night we use the Swordfish for attacks on shipping. A magnificent weapon. It can carry bombs, torpedoes or mines. As a torpedo carrier the Swordfish is superb. On more than one occasion the Swordfish have destroyed entire convoys on their way to Tripoli.

'When we await the return of the Swordfish, it is never, "Did you manage to get one?", it is always, "How many?". Torpedo work is a job for the expert. You may imagine flying over the sea on a dark night at about 100ft and not more than 400yd from the target. All that demands not only a high degree of skill, but a very high degree of courage. We owe a tremendous amount to the gallantry of our Swordfish crews who have done much determined and gallant work from this island.'

Above:
The Messerschmitt Bf109 attack on Acting Sub-Lt C. R. J. Coxon RN.

RED SEA SAGA

After missing the action at Taranto due to bomb damage, *Eagle* was ready for sea again by 16 November, and between then and the middle of March 1941 she was involved in various actions and ferrying aircraft to Malta. In March *Formidable* arrived to relieve *Eagle*, her aircraft having made strikes against enemy positions in East Africa on her way up the coast of Africa and through the Suez Canal. *Eagle's* Squadrons, 813 and 824, were ashore at Dekheila and waiting to rejoin the carrier to transit the Suez Canal into the Red Sea. However, enemy air-laid mines made the Canal impassable.

This was the position in mid-March when Cdr C. Keighley-Peach, then Commander (Flying) aboard *Eagle*, was sent for and told that an operation against Italian destroyers in the Red Sea was called for, probably in support of the Commonwealth troops which would by then have pushed as far as the coast. Keighley-Peach was told that any delay would be detrimental to the outcome of the East African campaign and he was instructed forthwith to fly all available Swordfish to Port Sudan and to seek out and destroy a number of Italian destroyers, and possibly a submarine, which were operating from their base at Massawa, about 300 miles south of Port Sudan. Keighley-Peach has described the situation:

'With the exception of fuel and bombs, which were to be supplied by the RAF, our party was to be self-supporting, which entailed carrying spares of all kinds, personnel and baggage with us.

When we departed from Dekheila we must have presented a quite astonishing spectacle to those left behind us. Each of the 17 Swordfish had some large spare part attached to the outside of the fuselage or between the wheels (a la torpedo): spare propellers, wheels, tool boxes — and personal luggage. One bright individual asked permission to take along his bicycle, as he thought it might be useful for running messages. Although I sympathised in principle, his request had to be refused. The passengers also presented something of a problem — the proportion of maintenance personnel, observers, telegraphist air gunners, and spare pilots that should be taken.'

One of those fortunate enough to be picked was TAG E. W. 'Ginger' Tyler, who remembers the trip vividly:
'I was serving with 813 Squadron at that time and there had been plenty of rumours about moves as usual but this one came as a bit of a surprise. On 25 March, 17 Swordfish took-off from Dekheila for Port Sudan, my aircraft being L7657 with Lt Sedgewick piloting and Mid Barringer as observer. First stop was at Assiut (now spelt Asyut) after following the Nile from Alexandria for two and a half hours. Here we refuelled and took-off again on the next leg to Aswan where we refuelled again and left for Wadi Halfa where we landed after six hours fifty minutes flying in very hot, tiring and boring conditions. When the squadrons took-off next day I

was left behind with K4018 which had developed an engine fault'.

This was Keighley-Peach's aircraft, as he recorded:
'It was here that we met with our only setback. My engine had been losing revolutions at the latter end of the journey, and it was decided to change a cylinder'.

'Ginger' Tyler continues:
'On the 27th we took-off with an air mechanic as passenger, my pilot now being Sub-Lt Timbs. We headed for Number 6 station landing strip along the Sudan railway, then on to Number 10 station where we picked up oil for our (still) ailing engine. The engine was burning oil at a tremendous rate. At the stations we had to haul drums of oil from the depot stores and refill the aircraft by hand, no easy job in such sweltering heat. The day ended with our arrival at Atbara, where accommodation was found for us with the small RAF contingent there. The temperature there at 16.30hrs was 105° in the shade. The next day, after some tinkering with the engine by RAF mechanics, we left for Port Sudan where we arrived after a three-hour flight. In the three days we had flown 1,300 miles, about a thousand of which was following the Nile. It was very boring at times, especially crossing the desert. Squadron personnel were first accommodated at a former girls' school in the town and we had to travel out to the aerodrome to work on the aircraft, but later we were allocated a large Nissen hut on the aerodrome.

'Operations were carried out daily with single aircraft flying down to the area around Massawa to keep tabs on the enemy ships. I went down in L7657 with Mid Sergeant as pilot and Lt Lyle as observer on 1 April. We landed at Mersa Taclai for fuel and then proceeded on down to Massawa. On this occasion we sighted an enemy destroyer just outside the port and shadowed him for some time, signalling reports back to base all the time. However, it being too late in the day for a striking force to intervene, we watched the ship go into harbour, then left for Mersa Taclai and eventually Port Sudan, after a day in which we spent over eight and a half hours in the air!'

Keighley-Peach carries on:
'On 2 April a high priority signal arrived from Aden to say that three Italian destroyers in Massawa dockyard were raising steam. This meant that at high speed it would be possible for these ships to be off Port Sudan by first light the next morning. On that basis, patrols were arranged with aircraft armed with six 250lb bombs. I took it upon myself to undertake the initial sortie, and at 05.45 the following morning I was out over the Red Sea, the cloud level being very patchy at around 1,500ft. My observer on this occasion was a splendid Warrant Officer named Wallington who, because we were not carrying a TAG, was also doing the communication work. Down below me I observed through the wispy cloud a destroyer steering roughly north and parallel to the coastline. She appeared to be going very fast by the amount of funnel smoke she was emitting. I told Wallington to "whistle up" the standby aircraft and that we were going down to attack. Not being a trained bomber pilot, I then proceeded to make a complete travesty of it. There was only spasmodic flak coming up and I released my bombs at about 500ft and dead in-line from astern — but too early, alas. The last bomb almost reached the target, but not quite, and the ship sailed onward, undamaged. Very unhappy with my effort, I then headed straight for home and the Ops Room, where I thought I had better remain. By this time more aircraft were on their way out and shortly afterwards a young pilot — Acting Sub-Lt (A) H. Sergeant RNVR — did precisely what I should have done and sank my target in quick time.'

This was only one of four Italian destroyers heading towards Port Sudan, and 'Ginger' Tyler continues the story:
'The ships were sighted very soon after take-off and looked as if they were coming in to bombard the port. All the Swordfish immediately dived in to attack with Mid Sergeant scoring five hits out of six and the destroyer just disintegrated; this turned out to be the *Nazario Sauro*. Sub-Lt (A) A. Suthers then made an attack and recorded in his logbook, "Attacked destroyer *Daniele Manin* — 2 hits, 1 near miss, destroyer later sank". The other two destroyers, *Pantera* and *Tigre*, were damaged so that they had to be run aground where they were finished off by gunfire. On returning from this sortie I had to go off again in P4070 with Lt Wellham and Sub-Lt Paine to shadow the two remaining destroyers and report their positions. As I mentioned, these were

damaged and driven ashore at Jedda. A few days later Kingston visited the two stranded destroyers and reported that the decks of both ships were strewn with dead sailors from our bombing and machine-gunning. They presented *Eagle* with the ensign from *Pantera* as a memento. Both Mid Sergeant and Sub-Lt Suthers were awarded the DSC for their part in the action. On 7 April, I was again on recce around Massawa but didn't see much so we flew across to some islands some way from the port and found a lagoon with about a dozen large ships anchored there, some afloat, but a number of them scuttled and resting on the bottom. Then we sighted a naval launch going away from a sinking ship — apparently the scuttling party. We immediately went in to attack, the pilot, Lt Slee, firing with his front gun, and, as we pulled out of the dive, I made use of my trusty Lewis gun. In all we made about three attacks and after the last one the launch had disappeared — probably sunk. The following day it was back to Massawa again but the port had surrendered and the only ship was an enemy hospital ship. During the day however one of our Swordfish had caught the torpedo boat *Giovanni Acerbi* in the harbour and bombed her, which resulted in another scuttling. The *Eagle* finally arrived off Port Sudan on 18 April and we flew aboard the next day. We then proceeded southward to Mombassa, Durban, St Helena and eventually to operate in the South Atlantic.'

The area also has many memories for Canon R. G. Chaffey-Moore, as he remembers those halcyon days:
'I was a RAF Padre in the Mombassa area during 1943 and some of 1944. Our HQ was at Port Reitz with 209 Squadron operating Catalinas and Sunderlands out of the harbour. I remember there was supposed to be a Jap submarine operating off the coast with a small spotter plane on board, so units were established all along the coast and on the islands.

'I spent much of my time flying around in a Sunderland visiting the lads. I always enjoyed going to the Seychelles as the plane invariably broke down and we enjoyed a few days' sailing. Returning one time, I looked up to see one of the crew open the rear door and throw the anchor out. This seemed strange as we were still at a considerable height and only halfway back. He then proceeded to throw out the baggage and pointed to the porthole. I looked out to see oil streaming from the engine — and then watched him unscrew anything surplus to our needs and throw that out until we were sitting on the floor. We entered Mombassa harbour just skimming the waves.

'One day my CO asked me, when next visiting Mogadishu, which was in Italian Somaliland, to bring back a case of gin for a mess party. At that time the campaign in that area was over. As far as I remember we flew up to Mogadishu in what was called a Stringbag, because on take-off, we were so low we hit the top of a palm tree and coconuts went flying in all directions. Anyway, we got there and I was put up in the Italian sergeants' mess, a most palatial place, decorated throughout in marble. The officers' mess had been so close to the runway that the RAF pulled it down. I couldn't get a ride back with the case so hitched a ride to Nairobi in a Dakota, and we had to hold back for a time as General Smuts was just arriving by air. The Fleet Air Arm offered to run me back but in order to accommodate me in the Swordfish I had to rest the case of gin on my stomach, not a very comfortable ride at the speed we were going. When we got back I had a quick shower and joined the officers in the mess to find the case being opened and remarks being made about a bottle of Curacao on the top. "We never ordered that", said the CO. "No", I replied, "It was a personal present from the Itai and I'm wishing to share it with you." Glasses were filled and we all toasted the success of the party to which all the top brass, civilian and service, had been invited. The RAF doctor, a bottle-a-day man, downed his and asked for another. In a moment he was on the floor, stiff as a board. Everyone stood around horrified and quickly placed their glasses on the bar. Someone was sent to ring up the naval doctor who was due to attend the party and on arrival said, "What have you boys been drinking?", then taking up the bottle sniffed and said, "Wood alcohol" and flung it into the lagoon. The RAF doctor fortunately recovered, but I doubt if you will find many who travelled in a Swordfish with a case of gin on their chest.'

`AT THE DISPOSAL OF COASTAL COMMAND´

One of the least desirable tasks that some Swordfish squadrons found themselves undertaking was operating under the control of RAF Coastal Command. The duties were either very boring, such as convoy patrols, or highly exciting (and dangerous), such as dive-bombing enemy positions. It is interesting to note that Coastal Command made use of Swordfish before the war and was still making use of them when the Germans surrendered in 1945.

As early as April 1940, a squadron of Swordfish had been made available to Coastal Command to carry out minelaying operations, but it was the swift movement of the German forces through the Low Countries that found Coastal Command seriously short of operational aircraft. An appeal was made to the Fleet Air Arm via the Admiralty and by the end of May no less than eight FAA squadron commanders had received a signal which said that they were to put themselves 'At the disposal of Coastal Command'. These were 812, 815, 818, 825 and 829 Squadrons, operating Swordfish, 801 and 806 Squadrons with Skua and Roc aircraft, and 826 Squadron with the first Albacores. The main bases to be used were Manston and Detling in Kent, North Coates in Lincolnshire, Bircham Newton in Norfolk and Thorney Island near Portsmouth. Over the next few

months their duties included convoy protection and dive-bombing military targets such as tanks, gun positions, vehicle convoys, shipping, barges and E-boats. The bombing raids were carried out in daylight and were extremely hazardous: in fact on one occasion a squadron of 12 Swordfish was found by marauding Bf109s and reduced in number to five. At night the Swordfish crews could get a bit of their own back, giving little respite to the enemy by bombing ports, airfields, power stations and fuel dumps, or mining Dutch, Belgian or even German harbours, estuaries and waterways.

J. K. Cannon, a sub-lieutenant serving with 825 Squadron at that time, remembers a few harrowing days:
'The squadron flew from Worthy Down to Detling on 18 May 1940 — I was flying Swordfish K8351 with Sub-Lt Berrill as observer and Naval Airman Brown as TAG. Two days later, before five in the morning, we flew to Bircham Newton for some operation or other that did not come off, and then returned to Detling that night. On 22 May we carried out an anti-submarine patrol over the North Sea, returning after two and a half hours — frozen. The squadron flew into action on 24 May when I, with Petty Officer Parker as observer, made daylight dive-bombing attacks on enemy tanks on the Calais-Gravelines road, receiving light flak through both

port wings. The following day it was a dive-bombing attack on motor vehicles along the Gravelines-St Folguin road. On 27 May we were detailed to co-operate (protect?) supply dropping Lysanders and then went to bomb enemy forces that were bombarding Calais. The CO of 825 at that time was Lt-Cdr Esmonde and he pressed home the attacks regardless of the odds. The following day I was detailed to search for MTBs and was shot up for my trouble in the starboard mainplane, and I very nearly flew into a balloon barrage when returning after over three hours in the air. With the evacuation taking place at Dunkirk the enemy forces were stepping up their hampering operations and on 29 May I dive-bombed various positions in an effort to reduce the problem. Two days later the squadron flew back to Worthy Down but that wasn't my last operational flying in Swordfish under Coastal Command. On the night of 1 July, in L7659 I carried out a night attack on enemy barges near Rotterdam and on the nights of 3 and 4 July laid mines in the Scheld estuary.'

The barges referred to were collected together for the invasion of the UK, and a concerned British Government ordered numerous air raids by the RAF and FAA to sink as many as possible. R. W. Slater, later to become CO of 836 Squadron, recalls his own trip to Rotterdam:

'Soon after the fall of France my squadron of 12 Swordfish were ordered to an airfield in Kent. We were told to put ourselves at the disposal of RAF Coastal Command. We arrived at Detling around lunch time and were told that mine-laying somewhere off the Dutch coast was to be our night's work, so we spent the whole afternoon getting the mines on, then just as we had finished, orders came through cancelling the mining and telling us to get bombed up for a visit to Rotterdam to try and sink the invasion barges which a reconnaissance aircraft had reported were accumulating in the river just west of the town.

'The squadron was divided into two waves, the first taking off 20 minutes before the second. It was a cloudy, dark night when we set out, but over the sea the weather cleared and we climbed to our operational height. As we crossed the enemy coast a thin layer of cloud was encountered about 2,000ft and stretching up to around 4,000ft, the last part of the journey being done by dead reckoning. As my observer told me that we ought to be just about there the first searchlights began showing and one or two balls of fire, probably flares, were shot up which lit the whole sky above the clouds. More and more searchlights came on but naturally could not pierce the cloud. We then went into line astern and I thought I would go down through the cloud and see if I could see the barges. However, when I got down through the cloud to around 2,000ft all was pitch black below, but I thought I saw the reflection of a light on some water, so quickly realised I was over the river and marked the spot, climbing up again with the intention of doing a decent dive-bombing attack. Just as I came out of cloud again the enemy opened fire and stuff came up all round us. I cursed myself for not letting the bombs go when I'd been down the first time. However, all went well and down we went and away went the bombs. My observer reported a large flash but otherwise could see no results due to the darkness. Personally I was too busy trying to shake off the searchlights as a climbing Swordfish is a pretty easy target to keep on, but after what seemed an interminable age we got back into cloud again and stayed in them until well over the sea.

'Breathing a sigh of relief we headed for home, only to find when we got there, England covered in a very low ground fog making it all look like the Thames estuary at low tide with the mud banks showing. My observer first thought we were over Harwich and told me to look for balloons. Then he thought we were over Deal where there were more balloons! I was so intent on looking for balloons in the dark that when suddenly there was a terrific jolt through the aircraft. I thought we had hit a cable and it was time to get out. However, glancing at my altimeter I saw it reading nought feet and realised we had hit the sea and bounced off it — so I am glad we didn't jump as it would only have been a 6ft fall and we would have looked rather stupid. By this time petrol was getting very low and it looked like being a rather uncomfortable end to our otherwise reasonably pleasant trip. Just after I switched over to my reserve gravity tank, which gave us another 20 minutes in the air, Margate pier was sighted and at last we knew where we were and flew home. We were the fourth and last of twelve aircraft to get back

actually to the aerodrome. The other members of the squadron had come down all over the place — one upside down in the Thames mud (the crew smelled horrible for days afterwards), another came down in a wood, another landed in a field and knocked the farmer up — only for him to think they were Germans and rang the police — a fourth crew also landed in a field and were rounded up by Royal Marines who didn't believe their story; the last crew to ring in and explain where they were, two young Sub-Lts, also landed in a field but when they knocked the owners up found two very pretty girls inside — they took a very long time indeed to report their whereabouts! Two Swordfish were lost that night we bombed the barges, shot down over the target area!'

John Pinkerton, a TAG, also came under Coastal Command control when 812 Squadron was used by the Command for a time:

'My experience of Swordfish flying started in May 1937 when I joined 812 Squadron aboard *Glorious*, and apart from a spell operating Swordfish float-planes from the battleship *Malaya*, I remained with the squadron until May 1941. During the years to April 1940 we of 812 served on *Glorious* with two other Swordfish Squadrons, 823 and 825, serving in the Mediterranean Sea and periodically operating from Dekheila — a shore base just outside Alexandria. A month after war was declared on

3 September 1939 the *Glorious* was detailed through the Suez Canal and Red Sea to the Gulf of Aden where we operated off the island of Socotra for some six to seven weeks to watch for the *Graf Spee* — reputed to be operating in the Indian Ocean — but we saw no sign of her. After crossing the Indian Ocean we arrived in Colombo, Ceylon, or Sri Lanka as it is now. Here we exercised for three or four weeks before sailing for Malta. The CO of the squadron at this time was Lt-Cdr Crawford, most of my flying being with Lt Harding in Swordfish L9761 'A' of X Flight. We flew off to Hal Far on 17 January 1940 and after a spell ashore embarked to return to the UK as the *Glorious* was required for the Norwegian campaign. We arrived in the Clyde in the middle of April and on the 21st we flew off *Glorious* in the Forth of Clyde in a fairly dense fog with 825 and half of 823 Squadrons. We of 812 landed at Prestwick in Ayrshire, the other half of 823 Squadron remaining on board to act as an anti-submarine force when the ship went to Norwegian waters with RAF Hurricanes — these being assembled on board. 812 stayed at Prestwick exercising around the southern parts of Scotland before flying south on 1 May, arriving at Ford the following day. Some of us were due for (under normal circumstances) some six weeks' foreign leave, but we were eventually granted two weeks. After one week we were recalled to Ford and seconded to RAF Coastal Command,

Above:
The engine running, a pilot walks to his Swordfish of 812 Squadron for another sortie in support of RAF Coastal Command.
Fox Photos

flying up to North Coates on 11 May. Here long-range fuel tanks were fitted in the observer's cockpit and the aircraft used a two-man crew instead of three. Although this usually meant leaving the TAG behind it did increase the endurance of the Swordfish from around four hours to six and a half if required. For instance, on 21 July I flew with Sub-Lt Eborn in P4007 to lay mines [codename "Gardening"] at Shiermonnikoog, being in the air for five hours twenty minutes at night. Two days later I flew a three-hour anti-submarine patrol off Flamborough during the day in L9732 and that night spent four and a half hours minelaying at Texel in L2746 with a different pilot.

'Throughout August we flew nearly every day on convoy patrols, usually our patch was the Humber/Flamborough area and the boredom was relieved occasionally by a minelaying trip. Some of these were not without incident or humour. On 27 August we were sent to Detling in Kent for a minelaying operation. It had, however, been heavily bombed in the Battle of Britain and we were unable to go that night, spending our time on settees in the roofless sergeants' mess! The following morning we went into town and, being mistaken for Dutch naval survivors, we were feted and given a cinema show. We took-off that night and arrived at the entrance to Zeebrugge, where, at a given signal, we dropped our mines at the exact same time the

Germans switched on their searchlights — and a very pretty picture it made as 12 mines dropped from 12 Swordfish — the exact locations of them being recorded by the enemy!

'From September 1940 until April 1941 we were re-allocated to RAF Thorney Island for anti-submarine patrols and searches in the Channel and northern part of the Bay of Biscay. On 9 September we went on a raid which I am not sure we should have been on! I flew in L7654 piloted by Sub-Lt Sier on a daylight bombing attack on barge escorts just off Zeebrugge. We were supposed to have had Spitfire escort from Orfordness but this did not materialise and we carried out the raid without recording any hits or suffering any damage. A popular supposition at the time was that a phonetic error (on the telephone) was made resulting in a confusion of numbers between 812 and 22 (a RAF Beaufort squadron number also based at North Coates) as to the squadron selected to perform that particular operation. I'm still not sure whether we or the Beauforts should have gone — just thank God we were not intercepted by enemy fighters. The squadron returned to North Coates where the long-range tanks were removed and we returned to naval control, flying north to Campbeltown on 19 March 1941.'

It is not generally known that Swordfish did their bit on D-Day in 1944. One of

Left:
The Swordfish of No 119 Squadron peel off for a dive bombing attack. More often than not the Swordfish operated individually, attacking targets of opportunity. *IWM (CL2285)*

the TAGs, Tom Mogford, has recorded his impressions of that and other events and we were fortunate that he has allowed some extracts to be included in this book.

'Doubtlessly, many TAGs served with squadrons lent to the RAF for various tasks, I had two sessions with Coastal Command, the second of which was, as far as I know, unique in the length of time that an entire naval air squadron was loaned to the RAF. Life during that period was so totally different from anything we knew in the Navy that it is probably worth recording.

'After being on *Indomitable* and a spell at Lee-on-Solent, I was drafted early in 1943 to RAF Thorney Island to join 833 Squadron which was operating the Stringbag, of course. Minelaying was the main nocturnal occupation at Thorney, the idea being to creep up to the harbour entrance — usually Cherbourg or Le Havre — drop the thing and push off as quickly and quietly as possible, secure in the knowledge that the minesweepers would be out bright and early in the morning to take care of it. One of the events I can clearly remember was the day a fully loaded Hampden blew up at dispersal with quite spectacular results. After a few weeks we moved down to RAF St Eval where there was some talk of us mining the Brest area, but the idea came to nothing and we returned to the Navy. I then spent a short time ashore, a period in the escort carrier *Stalker* and finally a

spell in MAC ships. It was the end of May when we returned from an Atlantic crossing and we all went on leave — only to find the proverbial telegram, "Return RNAS Maydown forthwith". So, it was back to Maydown overnight to find my own crew already arrived, together with several other crews. Within a few hours we were on our way to RAF Manston. "Where the hell is Manston?", said a voice as we heaved our kitbags, hammocks and flying gear aboard the Dakota. "Dunno", somebody replied, "Sussex or Kent, I think, anyway, somewhere down south". Several hours later we arrived at Manston to join 819 Squadron. The Swordfish were already there, neatly lined up, painted matt black with three unfamiliar white stripes. It was then that the penny dropped, the date was 1 June 1944 and rumour had it that the invasion was about to begin. Our sister squadron turned up, 415 Squadron of the RAF, flying — believe it or not — Albacores. Heaven only knows at which aeronautical knacker's yard they had languished since they were discarded by 841 Squadron. There were many instances of Navy aircrew flying RAF aircraft but this is the only case I know of where the reverse applied. Their crews, needless to say, were not too happy with their elderly kites.

'Daylight operations started with 819 Squadron laying smoke screens around the original invasion convoys. I was airborne at 09.00hrs that morning in

Above:
**Swordfish of 816 Squadron,
painted up in invasion
stripes, out on a training
sortie; they were used in
support of Coastal
Command during the
Normandy landings.**
IWM (A24986)

Swordfish NE134 piloted by Sub-Lt
Patterson to lay our smoke screen;
thereafter, June was a busy month for
me. We put down other smoke screens to
cover the Channel convoys on six
occasions. On the night of the 11th we
went out on a night anti-shipping patrol
and ended up dive-bombing three
E-boats off Le Touquet and a fortnight
later it was E-boats again but off
Dunkirk. At night anything that moved
in the Channel was duly duffed up, in an
area ranging from the coast of
Normandy in the south to the Hook of
Holland in the north. Sometimes worth-
while targets were illuminated with
flares for the Beaufighters. Strangely,
the Stringbags and Beaufighters proved
to be quite a successful combination. On
the night of 29 June we were flying in
NF131 'K' when we found 14 E/R-boats
going east at about 20kt. We attacked
down to 2,000ft but the bombs were
observed to fall between two vessels. We
had eight Swordfish out that night and
seven made attacks on enemy shipping.

'Manston was one of the busiest bases
in the South of England and many
shot-up and crippled aircraft were
diverted there for emergency landings.
It is a sad fact that one grew hardened to
them and I find it most alarming now to
recall just how dispassionately one

could view a crashing aircraft — providing of course that you weren't in it
yourself! Fortunately there were some
happy outcomes and even comical ones
— like the Polish fighter pilot out of
nearby Hawkinge who put his Spitfire
— spewing clouds of smoke — down
hard and very fast on the grass in front
of our dispersal and cheerfully apolo-
gised for his rather hectic arrival with
the simple explanation, "My oil — she
boil". Characters abound in wartime and
we had our share. Such was the distance
between dispersal, mess and living
quarters that Manston, in common with
most RAF airfields, was liberally supplied with bicycles which we made full
use of. One of our TAGs, best left
unnamed, rapidly achieved fame as the
world's worst cyclist. Whilst just about
capable of staying aboard the machine
in motion, he proved to be utterly
incapable of stopping the thing. The
loud crash that heralded his arrival at
the crewroom every morning became an
event not to be missed. Our lad could be
found, absolutely unperturbed, picking
himself and machine up from the
tarmac. In time he perfected his tech-
nique by simply cannoning off any
handy reasonably soft object nearby,
snooker fashion.

'Almost every conceivable type of
Allied aircraft used Manston at some
time or another during the invasion
period. Perhaps the strangest of them
all, and humorous, were the two that
arrived one night late in June 1944. In
the small hours of the morning two
aircraft — both burning navigation
lights — joined the circuit and, despite
the lack of R/T contact, the control tower
staff, rather naively, illuminated the
duty runway. The unknown aircraft
promptly landed, then . . . silence! For a
long time nothing happened so the
crash crew were alerted and despatched
to ascertain the whereabouts of the new
arrivals. After a search they found two
brand-new Bf109s of the very latest
type, complete with pilots. Once over the
shock the duty corporal contacted the
tower and the authorities swung into
action, carting the pilots off to the
guardroom and hauling the 109s away
from the runway to a position near the
tower. Peace and quiet then prevailed
until, at the first glimmer of dawn in the
east, a Stringbag came trundling
around the perimeter track, back from
patrol, the weary crew looking forward
to their bacon and eggs. As it
approached the tower the Swordfish

came to an abrupt halt: the pilot, well up on his aircraft recognition, had spotted the outline of the 109s. An earnest and rather heated discussion then took place between the now thoroughly alarmed pilot and his navigator. Both were convinced that they had mistaken the North Foreland for Cap Gris-Nez and landed in occupied France — how else could you account for 109s parked near the tower? Even the TAG was by this time wide awake, sitting up and taking notice. At the very point of turning the aircraft and legging it back to the runway to attempt a take-off, the panic was allayed by the familiar sight of a Hillman utility truck arriving at the tower. A relieved but still shaky Stringbag crew then continued on to dispersal. We were never told if the German pilots had put down at Manston in error, mistaking the North Foreland for Cap Gris-Nez, and Manston for the airfields of Abbeville or St Omer, or, seeing very little future in the Luftwaffe at that time, had deliberately surrendered. Within a couple of days both aircraft had British markings painted on and were duly flown to Farnborough.

'At the end of July we were on the move again. The flying-bombs were causing real trouble and defence against them took priority. An extra couple of Typhoon squadrons were moved in to deal with them and, accordingly, we had to go. We moved to a grass strip near Folkestone called Swingfield and its austerity came as a bit of a shock after the comforts of a big base. Entirely under canvas, a tent was no protection against the flying-bombs which regularly whistled over. At first the crew tent would empty rapidly as we rushed out to goof, but eventually the novelty wore off and, whilst not actually ignoring them, we stayed put and hoped that they would keep going, which they usually did. At dusk one evening, in Swordfish NE999, we were just passing Dover at around 800ft on our way out for an anti-submarine patrol when the sky was suddenly full of buzz-bombs. Some dozen or so of the things passed above and either side of us in the space of two minutes. It was an attempt to flood the defences and every gun for miles around was letting rip. The old Stringbag sailed blithely through it all without a scratch, not surprising really as it would take a very thick ack-ack gunner to mistake a Stringbag — bogging along fully loaded at some 75kt — with a doodlebug! That wasn't the only time: I

see from my logbook that on 24 July I recorded that "Another patrol dodging doodlebugs" and on the 28th, "No shipping — lots of flying bombs!".

'For over two months at Swingfield it was much the mixture as before and it was well into October that they pulled us out of the mudheap that the strip had become. Our days and nights were spent on laying smoke screens for Channel convoys by day and flare-dropping over enemy ships at night. On 17 August we illuminated a convoy off Cap Gris-Nez for Beaufighters after attacking two E-boats ourselves off Ostend — then attacked the convoy ourselves after the Beaufighters had gone, quite a night. We moved up to Bircham Newton in Norfolk, a couple of Stringbags being left at Biggin Hill for a week or so in case of emergencies. At Bircham we had a spot of leave as the overdue major inspections of the aircraft were carried out. When we returned from leave we were issued with khaki battledress, a Smith and Wesson .38 revolver and holster, which only strenthened 415's claim that we were a bit of a cowboy outfit anyway . . . The squadron left for the continent on 9 November, landing at St Crioux in Belgium to form No 142 GR Wing of the 2nd Tactical Air Force. Three days later we flew in to Maldagem, a large ex-Luftwaffe base. I found it somewhat unnerving to move on to an airfield which a few days before had housed the Germans. Discarded tools and equipment lay everywhere, clothing, personal effects such as letters by the hundred. One particular letter I remember was to a Sgt W. Kipper from Frau Kipper, and was giving Willi a monumental rollocking. "There was Willi", it read, "living on the fat of the land in perfect safety, no doubt up to all sorts of tricks with the French and Belgian girls, while she, Helga Kipper and her mother, were stuck in Hamburg with all the bombing, the food shortage, the housing shortage . . . etc, etc". We all felt a bit sorry for poor old Willi.

'Operations from Belgium were almost always to the north for by this time, late 1944, things were fairly quiet in the south. We covered all of the Belgian coast and most of the Dutch as well, our parish extending up to the Frisians, which was about the limit of the Stringbag's range. As usual, the aircraft's speed or lack of it caused problems. One crew, patrolling off the Hague, picked up a radar contact heading north. They made painfully

Right:
Members of 819 Squadron at RAF Swingfield, Kent, in August 1944. *T. Mogford*

slow progress and it took a considerable amount of time to close the fast-moving target, which they identified as a destroyer and attacked, claiming a hit. "Not possible", said the debriefing officer adamantly, "there are no enemy destroyers for miles around". Fortunately, photo-recce pictures taken the following day showed a destroyer beached near Ijmuiden. It turned out that a new destroyer, nearing completion in a Dutch yard for the German Navy, was forced to evacuate under cover of darkness as the Allies drew near. Although unarmed it was capable of 35kt which, together with the 20kt headwind against the Swordfish, was the reason for the prolonged slog to catch up.

'Winter during 1944/45 was pretty severe and it was a constant battle to keep warm in the spartan quarters we occupied. Luckily leave was frequent now and well organised, travel to UK usually being by Transport Command aircraft from Antwerp to Northolt or, if the weather was constantly bad, by RAF high-speed launch from Ostend to Dover. Occasionally we could go via Bircham Newton if the aircraft was due for a major inspection. I remember one such instance, just before Christmas, that six aircraft left for the UK on a particularly filthy day. There was fog, heavy snow, the lot! We delayed departure but eventually took a chance and set out. The weather over the Channel got worse and the first available airfield to get in to turned out to be the American base at Halesworth in Suffolk. What complicated things was the 20 or so Mustangs and Thunderbolts all milling round the circuit with the same idea as ourselves. Most of them had been to Berlin that day and were critically low on fuel. Somehow the tower sorted

things out and everyone landed, but more and more fighters were arriving with the base gradually getting packed with aircraft from all over the South of England. That was one night when four British TAGs spent the night in the officers' mess with our own crews and some two dozen assorted Mustang and Thunderbolt pilots. We returned to Maldagem on 12 December in LS420 and went back to anti-shipping patrols. By now there was relatively little shipping to be seen but on the night of 29 December we did observe V2 rockets being fired from the Hook of Holland. Which reminds me of another story. Operating from Belgium we quickly became aware of the flak ships that used to anchor off the Hook of Holland from dusk to dawn. Sometimes there were three, but more often four of them. We often had a pop at them but their gunners were a pretty trigger-happy lot liable to cut loose at anything in range. They seemed to pay special attention to us so it paid to be cautious, for it soon became obvious they knew the sound of a Pegasus. If we came back from a patrol with a full load it became routine to unload them on these ships rather than carry them home. They soon became known as "The Four Horsemen of The Hook" and CPO Jackie Wayles drew a cartoon of a group of German sailors, complete with "Four Horsemen" cap ribbons, complaining to an admiral about the "Verdamnt Swordfish". Despite a large expenditure by both sides of bombs and cannon shell, they never hit us and, as far as I know, we never hit them. Early in the new year we moved to Knocke Le Zoute on the coast and on 15 January attacked five enemy ships off the coast of Holland

'Early in February, rumours that we were soon to be withdrawn were confirmed. Unluckily on 13 February, the night of the big squadron farewell knees-up, I was on stand-by. Now, at Knocke we were living in some style in the Golf and Memlinke hotels which boasted all mod cons — in fact I was sharing the bridal suite! Lulled into a false sense of security by a period of quiet nights I stuck my head in the party "to see how things were going". That was a mistake. Some hours later, having entered into the spirit of the thing, we were suddenly called out. To this day I can't recall events too clearly. My logbook for that night, my last operational trip with 819, and in a Swordfish, reads — "NE999 Anti-shipping patrol. Caught in heavy flak, chased by Ju88 nightfighter". The trip remains for ever just a blur — probably just as well.

'On 26 February 1945 the ground-crews boarded a TLC at Ostend and the squadron took off for Bircham Newton, leaving the Albacores to go it alone. We heard later that they suffered some losses after we had gone. At Bircham it was just a case of waiting until the day the CPO stuck his head round the door and said, "Clear out your aircraft lads, they'll be going tomorrow". We wandered down to dispersal and I hauled myself up into NE999 to clear out the bits and pieces that gather in the rear cockpit, then sauntered back slowly to the mess. I didn't realise she was the last Swordfish I would climb into, now I wish I had lingered a while longer for, like all her kind, she was a great lady.'

As 819 Squadron returned to the UK, some of its tasks fell on another Swordfish unit — No 119 Squadron which had been formed up from a Flight of No 415 (RCAF) Squadron, but at that time operating the Albacore. The new squadron came under No 155 GR Wing at Manston but operated out of Bircham Newton when in the UK or airfield B83 in Belgium, better known as Knocke Le Zoute. The CO was Sqn Ldr J. I. J. Davies DFC, who must have wondered what he had done wrong to get command of a squadron of biplanes. The first Swordfish arrived in January 1945 and the first operational patrol was carried out by Flg Off Rabbets on 6 February. The Swordfish were used for day and night patrols, looking for troublesome E-boats or midget submarines. By the end of March four midget submarines had been sunk, and

three E-boats and some other craft damaged. The squadron got a new CO, Sqn Ldr N. Williamson, who took off on 4 May with Flt Lt D. G. Matkin as navigator for a patrol. At 14.30hrs they found a midget submarine apparently stranded on a sandbank. They could see no sign of a crew and, realising that the depth charges were useless for such an attack, they flew back to base and changed them for bombs. An attack was made and oil was seen to spread out on the sea — this was the incident widely referred to in other publications as the midget submarine attacked only 3½ hours before Germany surrendered. A few other patrols were flown, but soon it was all over and on 22 May 1945 the squadron flew 14 Swordfish back across the Channel to land at Bircham Newton.

SWORDFISH OVER MADAGASCAR

When *Illustrious* returned from repairs in the USA her first role was to support the amphibious assault on the Vichy-controlled island of Madagascar in the Indian Ocean. This was an essential step as it would then be denied to the Japanese who, it was felt, might be allowed by the French authorities to set up a base there.

Illustrious left the Clyde on 23 March 1942, to join Force F based at Freetown in West Africa. Just before arriving, however, she suffered a hangar fire in which 10 Swordfish and one Fulmar were destroyed. The fire apparently started from spontaneous combustion of some camouflage netting that was stored in the hangar roof; in any case Freetown managed to make up the loss. Force F, under the command of Rear-Adm E. N. Syfret CB, also included *Formidable*, and she was to be responsible for attacking the Madagascan airfields and protecting the fleet. On board she had 12 Fulmars of 800 and 806 Squadrons, nine Sea Hurricanes of 880, and 24 Albacores of 827 and 831 Squadrons, while the aircraft complement on *Illustrious* was 20 Swordfish of 810 and 829 Squadrons, one Fulmar of 806 for night-fighter duties, and 20 Martlets of 881 and 882 Squadrons. The latter's aircraft were to neutralise any naval forces and support the ground forces. The whole operation was code-named 'Ironclad'.

At 03.44hrs on 5 May 1942, *Illustrious* launched 18 Swordfish, followed by eight Martlets, to attack Vichy warships in Diego Suarez harbour. The operations were successful, the only incidents of note being the loss of one Swordfish and one Albacore. The former was DK788 '2A' of 810 Squadron and, ironically, the mount of the CO, Lt R. N. Everett RN, and his observer, Sub-Lt (A) J. H. G. Tapscott and TAG Petty Officer R. J. Groves. His aircraft hit by anti-aircraft fire, Lt Everett managed to ditch close to the shore but turned it over, and the crew was taken prisoner. All were released when Allied forces overran the area including the town of Antsirane. The island was firmly in British control by 7 May, after 59 Swordfish sorties and the loss of four aircraft, other losses being a Fulmar and a Martlet. In return, an armed merchant cruiser — *Bougainville* — and two submarines — *Le Heros* and *Beveziers* — had been sunk by 829 Squadron, and 881 Squadron had shot down three Potez 63.11 reconnaissance aircraft and four Morane Saulnier MS406C fighters. Both carriers entered the captured harbour on 9 May and remained there until the 20th.

A second series of operations was planned later in 1942, because the southern part of the island was still in Vichy hands. For this trip only *Illustrious* was available and she embarked

810 and 829 Squadrons with 18 Swordfish, 806 with six Fulmars and 881 with 12 Martlets. The ship left Mombassa on 5 September to take part in Operation 'Stream', the landings at Majunga on 10 and 11 September, her main tasks being to provide reconnaissance and showing the flag. Operation 'Jane' followed on 18 September, with more shows of strength around Tamatave, though there were only 57 sorties over the three days of operations. The same day, the 18th, *Illustrious* left for Durban and a short refit.

CAMARADES DE L'AIR

SI nous nous trouvons forcés de faire sauter votre matériel, c'est pour éviter à ce que, par conception de discipline mal comprise, des vies précieuses ne soient perdues. En Syrie, de nombreux aviateurs français, qui au début nous ont combattus, sont maintenant dans l'aviation française libre, et contribuent à la destruction des Allemands en Afrique du Nord.

Il se peut qu'il y ait des agents conscients ou inconscients de l'ennemi qui essayent de vous exciter à commettre des actes nuisibles à la cause des Alliés, donc aux intérêts de la France. Vous leur demanderez des nouvelles des aviateurs de l'Indochine, qui, la rage au cœur, doivent regarder les Japonais régner en maîtres et les empêcher de s'approcher de leurs appareils. S'ils s'obstinent, vous saurez les empêcher de faire du mal.

Nous promettons solennellement aux aviateurs qui veulent continuer la lutte les meilleurs des appareils de la R.A.F. Vous pourrez ainsi continuer la lutte et contribuer à la revanche que les ailes françaises ont commencé à prendre dans les cieux de la Manche et de l'Afrique du Nord.

IMPORTANT: VOIR AU VERSO ➡

FRANÇAIS DE MADAGASCAR

Des forces importantes britanniques sont en train de débarquer chez vous

— **VOICI POURQUOI:** —

LE Japon, aux ordres de Hitler, apporta la guerre à l'Orient. Les opérations dans le Pacifique ont démontré que le plan japonais est de s'emparer de toutes les bases stratégiques. La souveraineté territoriale n'y compte pour rien.

Se servant des mêmes méthodes, les Japonais essayent de faire dans le Pacifique et dans l'Océan Indien ce que les allemands ont fait en Europe.

Ils comptent surtout sur l'hésitation des Alliés de se servir de ces mêmes méthodes pour leur permettre de faire abus de la faiblesse, de l'indécision et de la neutralité.

Mais nous avons trop bien appris les leçons de la guerre totale en Europe pour rester dupe de l'Axe.

Vichy a espéré rester neutre. Le résultat en est que l'Indochine est devenue la plus importante base d'opérations japonaises contre les Alliés. Les Français d'Indochine, soumis à la domination la plus humiliante, nous blâment aujourd'hui de ne pas avoir paré à temps le coup japonais.

Nous venons chez vous précisément pour déjouer un coup pareil.

Nous n'avons aucun dessein territorial contre votre île. M. Churchill a solennellement déclaré que l'Empire Français restera intact.

Nous venons chez vous comme vos alliés. Nous croyons que vous nous accueillirez comme tels. Contre l'Axe nous sommes tous des alliés.

Seuls les complices ou les agents de l'Axe peuvent prétendre que nous sommes ici pour vous attaquer. Nous savons que la grande majorité d'entre vous voudrait reprendre la lutte à notre côté pour sauvegarder votre île et pour la libération de la France. Les autres seront repatriés ou pourront rester en toute liberté.

VIVE LA FRANCE !

IMPORTANT: VOIR AU VERSO ➡

Above:

The packed flight deck of *Illustrious*, with Martlets of 881 and 882 Squadrons, a Fulmar for night fighting and three Swordfish. The photograph was taken after the practice exercise for the invasion of Madagascar.

Cdr R. N. Everett

Left:

An example of leaflets dropped from Swordfish on the morning of 5 May 1940 during the invasion of Madagascar.

Right:
Lt R. N. Everett, on the left, was unfortunate enough to be shot down on the dawn strike against Diego Suarez. This shot on the deck of *Illustrious* **was taken with his crew.** *Cdr R. N. Everett*

Below right:
Lt Everett's Swordfish, DK788 '2A' of 810 Squadron, in the shallows after ditching. Shrapnel severed the fuel line and here you see ratings pinching anything reuseable from the wreck. *Cdr R. N. Everett*

Bottom:
Swordfish HS164 '2F' of 810 Squadron flying off the East African coast after the Madagascar strikes. *Cdr R. N. Everett*

Above:
Crews of 810 Squadron relax in the sunshine at Tanga, a shore base; Port Rietz was also used after the strikes on Diego Suarez. *Cdr R. N. Everett*

Left:
Even the natives were friendly! *H. Liddle*

Below:
Illustrious **sailed for Ceylon not long after the operations against Madagascar, and here a Swordfish is being refuelled from a bowser which was towed around by an elephant. The pace could be described as leisurely!**
IWM (A26739)

WORN WITH PRIDE

One in six Telegraphist Air Gunners (TAG) lost their lives during World War 2. Think about that for a moment as we recall that in the distant past the Admiralty had decreed that when flying from aircraft carriers a pilot had quite enough to do just flying the aircraft, so he needed a navigator (observer) to direct him and find the carrier again; also, as front armament and aircraft performance would be limited, it was essential to have rear cover in the form of an air gunner, who could also double-up as a radio operator. Eric Bond of the Telegraphist Air Gunners' Association gives an insight into their training and background:

'Before the outbreak of the Second World War in 1939 the selection of aircrew Telegraphist Air Gunners in the main came from the Communications Branch of the Royal Navy. During the war, volunteers for TAG duty were drawn from the Telegraphist, Seaman, Royal Marine and New Entry branches of the Royal Navy. The majority had joined for the period of hostilities and were termed "Hostilities Only" (HOs), although some came from the Royal Navy "Y" Entry Scheme. After the interview, educational tests, physical examination, etc, they went through basic training in Morse and wireless theory, the syllabus being: wireless telegraphy (W/T), radio telephony (R/T), wireless procedure, which included Fleet and Spotting procedures, coding and decoding, signals — flags and semaphore, Aldis lamp — RDF (Radar) operation, camera gun and aircraft

recognition, target-towing instruction and parachutes. These courses took place at the shore bases of HMS *Royal Arthur*, *St Vincent* or *Victory*. The successful ones were then drafted to the Air Gunners' School at RNAS Worthy Down (HMS *Kestrel*) near Winchester. Later in the war some trainees were sent to Canada to pass through No 1 Naval Air Gunners' School (NAGS). The trainees were then required to fly in a variety of aircraft for around 60 hours gaining experience in operating the Lewis, Vickers and Browning machine guns in air-to-air and air-to-ground gunnery exercises. On passing out from the Air Armament Training station at St Merryn (HMS *Vulture*) in Cornwall they became Acting Leading Airman, Acting Air Gunner 3rd Class. On being posted to a squadron they would then undergo operational training to bring them up to the standard required for combat flying. However, it was not until 1942 that the TAGs were awarded a flying badge to wear on their left cuff — an acknowledgement that was "Worn with pride".'

The exploits of the TAGs at war deserves a book of its own and space here only allows a glimpse of their contribution to the war fought in the air and at sea. During wartime, even under extreme circumstances, there is humour in adversity, as you will see:

'Ginger' Tyler

'On 3 December 1940 I was detached to Fuka in the Western Desert with three

Swordfish from 813 Squadron. A push against the Italians was rumoured. On the night of 7 December I flew with Lt Slee and his observer, Sub-Lt Bull, with a full complement of flares to drop over Maktila, a huge enemy stores depot. HMS *Terror* was lying offshore and as we stooged round dropping our flares, *Terror* carried out its plastering operation very successfully. We left the target after the bombardment with Maktila a mass of flames and exploding dumps. There was some AA fire but it was sporadic and we got back safely. The following night I returned to Maktila to give them a second dose but the bombardment was called off because our own troops were nearby. On this occasion the pilot was Lt Sedgewick but for some reason we did not carry an observer so a RAF fighter pilot came along for the ride. Now when I went on these trips I always took a steel helmet and when our RAF pilot queried this as I climbed in the aircraft he pooh-poohed my explanation that I was somewhat averse to having my butt punctured by ground fire — but it was a different story when we stooged over the target dropping flares and being fired at by the ground defences. He only experienced it for a short time as the bombardment was called off. When we returned to base he hopped out quickly, remarking that

that was enough for him, he didn't think much of the experience!'

Nat Gold

'As usual when going into action, there is fear of the unknown but once the action starts that fear goes and you are trying to do your job and get away without damage or injury. Once you are away from the danger a different feeling comes over you: elation, you feel great and it's a wonderful world, but that is after an op. My story starts during the late afternoon of Saturday 12 April 1941 when the squadron assembled for a briefing to attack enemy shipping with torpedoes. I found I would be flying with Mid Elwell whom I had flown with before and had confidence in. Lt-Cdr E. D. Howie would lead five torpedo-carrying Swordfish plus one carrying bombs of 830 Squadron to attack five Italian merchant ships escorted by three destroyers somewhere southwest of Pantellaria. We would be the last to attack. Great! One Swordfish went off early to search for and shadow the convoy. On leaving the briefing room, my room mate, Leading Airman Todd, confided that it was exactly a year to the day since he was shot down in a Skua over Norway.

'We took off and formed up as usual around Filfla and set course at 18.50hrs

Below:
The enclosed canopy of a Swordfish II, known sometimes as a Swordfish IV, identifies this aircraft as being from No 1 NAGS in Canada. This unit allowed TAGs to be trained out of the war zone for eventual form-up with the Lend-Lease-equipped squadrons in the USA.
Public Archives of Canada

On arriving over the convoy we received the signal to break formation and take up our attacking positions. To our amazement the first flare illuminated right alongside our Swordfish which encouraged a few guns to fire up at us. One round fascinated me, it appeared to look like a large Catherine wheel coming up at us. I had heard that there were guns that could fire a shell with flaying chains attached to it and I wondered if this was one. We did not wait to find out as we surged higher to get out of the way. It is a hair-raising experience sitting up top watching other aircraft attack and knowing that you are to be last — when the hornet's nest has been stirred up. We slowly lost height, the last flare had been dropped and we were almost in position when a destroyer appeared dead ahead pumping out thick black smoke. She was in an ideal position to be attacked, we couldn't miss, but our target was the supply ships. We passed very low over her and as we cleared the other side the flare went out putting everywhere in pitch darkness. We were very low down and Elwell banked to port just as a breeder gun on the destroyer opened fire. A stream of flaming onions came snaking across passing near the rudder, then the gunner proceeded to continue swishing about in the hope of hitting us and I could hear it crackling and popping past. Then another one

opened up sweeping over the starboard mainplane and just missing the engine. Just then, peering round the overload tank in the darkness, the stern of a ship suddenly loomed up. Midshipman Elwell reacted very quickly, he dropped the torpedo — which gave us a little extra lift — pulled back on the stick and we literally climbed up the stern of the ship. We climbed quickly away but no one else attempted to fire at us and we made our way to the rendezvous point just in time to tag on to the squadron as they formed up to fly back to Malta. When we got back there were two Swordfish missing — Petty Officer Charles Wines and his TAG, Leading Airman Edwards, who after dropping their torpedo were hit by fire almost continuously and crash-landed on the beach at Hammamet to be interned in Tunisia. Sub-Lt Dawson and my friend Todd were also lost that night, supporting his apprehension of events a year before; thankfully, they too were OK. That night we sank all five merchantmen and one destroyer — not a bad night's work.'

Jack Wayles
'I remember Alfie Marsh of 810 Squadron, then attached to *Courageous*. He once went up on an anti-submarine patrol and, for one reason or another, the Swordfish was airborne almost to the limit of its endurance. We were all a

bit concerned as time went on and gathered on the flight deck to meet him. By the time his machine had rolled to a stop, Alfie had also reached his limit, and, in leaping out to reach the island heads, he clean forgot to slip his G-string and hung ignominiously head downwards outside the cockpit. Being somewhat on the short side, poor Alfie couldn't reach upwards as far as the G-string slip mechanism, and we gathered round the rapidly reddening head to pass the time of day. He didn't appear to be in his usual chatty mood, and, in fact, seemed only able to bawl, "Slip my G-string, I'm busting". That at least appeared to be the message after we had compared notes — so we slipped his G-string and he fell on his head and wet himself . . .

'I also remember 27 November 1940 and my B Flight Petty Officer, Scouse Eccleshall, for on that day Force H was escorting an east-bound convoy carrying tanks and military stores. South-west of Sardinia the force met *Ramillies*, which was to take the convoy on to Alexandria. Before the escorts had parted, a Swordfish from *Ark Royal* out on a reconnaissance patrol signalled that it had sighted the Italian fleet south of Sardinia; it was composed of two battleships, six cruisers, and sixteen destroyers. Another Swordfish went out to relieve the shadowing aircraft and this followed the enemy fleet reporting every movement. As the enemy fleet were still well out of range it was decided to try and slow them down until *Renown* could open fire. This was to be the job of the Fleet Air Arm, so at 11am in brilliant sunlight we got eleven Stringbags off armed with Duplex torpedoes. After flying for about twenty minutes we sighted the Italian fleet steaming in two columns, the battleships screened by the destroyers. At 12.40 our Swordfish force attacked out of the sun and things got a bit hectic for a while. I was flying with the CO, Lt-Cdr Johnstone and his observer, Lt Shaw, so we were first in and the flak was pretty formidable. The destroyer screen was so close in that there was barely sea room for our "fish" to run and, to cap it all, when we broke away, the fleet turned with us and I'm sure some of them overtook and passed us! As the striking force turned away the TAGs sprayed the bridge of the destroyer or battleship nearest. In returning singly to the "Ark" a lone Swordfish appeared astern of us and, from a distance, appeared to have a great lump of fuselage hanging off. Puzzled by this we throttled back until it finally caught up with us, then we found that the "lumps" were nothing more than old Scouse standing on his seat solemnly practising semaphore . . .'

Humorous or not, wherever the FAA found itself in action, one could be sure the TAGs were involved. It wasn't always easy for them in the rear cockpit and perhaps it might be an idea to round the chapter off with a piece by Nat Gold, who seemed to have had his fair share of the action:

'During the late afternoon of Tuesday 18 March 1941, the Swordfish of 830 Squadron were being armed for a forthcoming night operation. During the day I had carried out the usual checks on the aircraft I was to fly in that night, radio, guns, ammo, flares, etc. At that time I had no idea who my pilot might be or what armament we would be carrying. After supper I dragged my unwilling feet across to the briefing room and a quick glance at the board, "GOLD" — pilot — Petty Officer Charles Wines — that was enough, I need not look at the armament, we would be carrying bombs. My heart sank, this was to be my first dive-bombing operation; five Swordfish would lay magnetic mines at the entrance to Tripoli harbour and three others would dive-bomb heavy ack-ack positions. In the past, out of three bombing aircraft we generally lost one, so my chances of survival were slim — the only reassuring thought being that Charles Wines was the best dive-bombing pilot on the squadron. The briefing room quickly filled, a loud babble of voices, the air thick with cigarette smoke. The CO arrived and went to his usual position, a hush fell in the room. "Gentlemen", he announced, "our target tonight is to mine the entrance of Tripoli harbour, take-off will be 22.00hrs". He then proceeded to discuss formation positions, heights each aircraft were to fly at over the rendezvous, plan of action, etc, while the observers checked weather and conditions for their plot, and the air gunners recorded call signs, recognition signal for the day, ground station call sign and so on. I also had a quick word with Charles Wines, mentioning that this was my first dive-bombing operation, but he told me not to worry and promised to bring me back. The CO mentioned that RAF Wellingtons would also high level bomb Tripoli

on the bottom of my harness. I plugged my earphone into the radio socket and switched on, everything OK, I then plugged in the Gosport tube so I could speak to the pilot. In the observer's seat was an unsightly overload petrol tank which gave us a much longer endurance. In my overall pocket I carried various sized rubber bungs to plug any holes that might appear in the tank.

'Charles Wines climbed into his cockpit and settled in, once he was plugged into the Gosport he yelled, "Everything OK?". I replied, "Yes, all ready". The groundcrew were fussing around, one banged on the side of the cockpit and yelled, "The best of luck". Another mechanic cranked the engine and yelled to Charles to switch on, the engine fired and coughed; another try, this time the engine roared into life. Charles carried out his various checks and waved to the mechanics to pull the wheel chocks away. We taxied into the take-off position and the engine roared out as we took off with six 250lb bombs and a full fuel load. Once airborne we banked to starboard to take up our rendezvous position over the rock protruding out of the sea south of Malta and known as Filfla. We flew round Filfla with our dimmed navigation lights on, once on course these would be switched off and replaced by two very dim mauve formation lights, one on the strut each side of the pilot's cockpit and a further dim white light on the tail. We now formed into a very tight "V" formation led by the CO, and Tripoli two hours 20 minutes in front of us. Transit height was 4,000ft.

'Arriving at the target the CO gave the signal to break formation and take up action stations. The mine-laying Swordfish would throttle back and glide to within 100ft of the sea and try to release the mine as near the harbour entrance as possible. Gliding down, sparks and flames belched out the exhaust and one imagined all of Africa could see the fireworks. Once the mine had gone the aircraft was banked over to starboard heading out to sea and throttle applied to the engine, hoping and praying it would respond. Suddenly Charles's voice came through the Gosport tube, "There it is, all nicely warmed up". I jumped up and peered round the side of the overload tank, my heart thumping. Low on the horizon I could see an illuminated area and this grew in size as we approached. As we flew in from the north we could see that all hell had been

Top:
This posed shot shows a young TAG to good effect as the crew check out their equipment prior to an anti-submarine patrol from the escort carrier *Battler*.
IWM (A21618)

Above:
A TAG checks his drums of ammo for his trusty Lewis prior to a flight in West Africa. Note the case collector bag.
IWM (A22309)

that night. A loud moan erupted; this meant the Wellingtons, being faster than the Swordfish, would take off after us and arrive before we got there, causing the enemy gun crews to keep up a continuous box barrage.

'At 21.00 hrs, in pitch darkness, the squadron transport arrived to take the aircrews to their respective aircraft, this transport being an old builders' wagon! The first thing I did was to walk round the front of the kite and check the wing lockings, I didn't want the wings folding back on me if a mechanic had forgotten to secure them properly. They were OK so I climbed aboard, stowed my parachute, secured my parachute harness and fixed the G-string to the hook let loose down below and Charles called up again, "There's a beautiful big ship in the middle of the harbour — I'm going after it". Charles turned south and then east to arrive over the box barrage and then suddenly the nose of the Swordfish dropped and we went into a vertical dive. Sitting on my seat meant that I was going downhill backwards and could not see a great deal. Thoughts were racing through my head when I received a very heavy blow in the stomach. I froze, and thought, "My God, I've been hit". It really hurt, I was scared to touch the area, then I plucked up courage and thought I had better find out the extent of the damage. I gingerly placed my hand over the area where it hurt — the first thing I touched was part of my parachute harness strapping, which appeared to be intact. I thought this is strange — felt around a little further: no sticky blood — nothing. It then occurred to me I had brought along an additional pan of ammunition which had been resting by the gun mounting. This had slipped off in our steep dive and belted me in the stomach. Let me tell you, a pan of 100 rounds of ammo is some considerable weight, particularly when it flew through the air.

'The dive seemed endless so I hooked my arm over the side of the cockpit and heaved myself up. The sight before my eyes frightened the life out of me. It was just like daylight, tracer from breeder guns coming up from all directions like a string of onions, some white, some green, and some red, fascinating to watch (lethal to meet), snaking their way up slowly at first, then gathering speed until they were rushing like an express train, swishing, crackling, popping, I could even smell them! I could only stand and watch as the gunners below moved their guns and arched the tracer around the sky, how they missed I shall never know, we were a sitting duck. I leaned further over the side looking down in the direction we were diving. The ship now looked enormous and I suddenly thought, has Charles been hit? Should I yell at him through the Gosport — no, that would only distract his concentration if he was alright, but, if he was wounded a yell might bring him round sufficiently to pull out of this headlong dive. As I arrived at these thoughts, all happening in seconds, my worries were answered as "G" pressure made me slump back in my seat, my whole body feeling like a ton weight. Then I heard a bomb

explode, followed by another, and another until I had accounted for all six — Charles had timed it beautifully. As the bombs exploded we banked away so I attempted to pull myself up again only to be subjected to more "G" forces as Charles threw the kite all over the sky to avoid the flak. Tracer from the breeder guns was still uncomfortably close and searchlights twisted across the sky in agitated anger because they could not locate us. Suddenly we were free — it seemed so quiet and peaceful after what we had been through. Running from the flak like a frightened rabbit, it felt as though we had entered our rabbit's warren into complete darkness. How we ever got away from that holocaust I shall never know — it was like standing in front of a firing squad and every bullet missing.

'Charles's voice yelled through the Gosport tube, "We got her, straddled her right across the foc's'le". I yelled back, "Bloody good show, but we were a bit low weren't we? What height did you pull out at?" Charles yelled back, "We commenced our dive at 4,000ft and pulled out at 800". Silence. We sighted the rendezvous flame float and flew across to join the other Swordfish as the CO gave the signal to return to Malta. As we flew back I wondered what damage our bombs would have done as each one had a blast rod screwed into the nose. This was approximately a foot long with a circular plate on the end. When the bomb hit the target the intention was for it to explode above ground level to cause the maximum blast effect. In retrospect, maybe we would have caused more penetrating damage without the rod. Charles yelled that we were back and the Swordfish banked over to join the circuit prior to landing. This could also be a worrying time as Jerry usually wandered around the area at night and dropped the occasional anti-personnel bomb. But we landed OK and after the engine had stopped I undid the straps of my helmet and pushed it back, savouring the cold air on my forehead, ears still ringing from the engine and radio noises. We had been flying for over five hours and as I walked back to the briefing room with Charles I had the wonderful feeling which only comes when your feet are on the firm earth after many hours of flying. One Swordfish was missing, and I learnt later that my pal, Bill Thomson, and his pilot had been interned in Tunisia.'

*The 'Breeder' machine gun quoted in this story was in fact manufactured by the Breda company which accounts for the nickname.

Above:
A TAG's rear eye view as a Swordfish from Hatston makes a practice bombing attack on a smoke float.

BISMARCK

Although the main text of this chapter is about the *Bismarck*, it is interesting to note that Swordfish carried out a number of torpedo strikes against German capital ships. The first, of which little is known, is remembered by Cdr John Stenning, then a lieutenant:

'During the summer of 1940, 821 and 823 Squadrons with 12 Swordfish each were based at RNAS Hatston. They carried out anti-E-boat and anti-submarine patrols more or less throughout the 24 hours of the day. At the same time three aircraft of each squadron were always on the tarmac armed with torpedoes, and the aircrews at readiness.

'On 21 June 1940 we got a call-out, it was just after *Scharnhorst* had sunk the *Glorious*. I was the senior of the three 821 Squadron pilots and although Lt J. C. "Cocky" Reed of 823 was senior to me, my observer, Lt V. A. T. Smith RAN, was senior to him — so I led the formation. Needless to say the two squadrons had never flown together before or carried out a joint attack. The aircraft had long range tanks in the observer's seat so each aircraft had either an observer or TAG. Lt Smith did the navigation for the flight.

'We took off at 12.45 and I was flying Swordfish P4144. As usual my logbook says nothing — "Height 1,500 to 8,000ft. To Utsire Islands and search north — torpedo attack on *Scharnhorst* and 7 destroyers — no hits, 2 a/c shot down." I really did conform to the order that no details are to be recorded in logs

in case the ship was sunk and such logbooks picked up by a U-boat! We flew to the Norwegian coast climbing in fairly open formation. It was a slow business as the aircraft with torpedo, long-range tanks and crew were a bit heavy for the power of the old Peggy engine. It took nearly two hours to climb to 8,000ft and reach the Norwegian coast, and we hit off our objective and turned north proceeding up the coast a few miles out to sea. After quite a short time we spotted *Scharnhorst* with a close escort of seven destroyers steaming south at high speed. I gave the hand signal for attack formation, pointing my thumb backwards for line astern. I stayed to the east of the enemy and Cocky led his sub-flight to the west.

'When the flak started it wasn't too accurate and once I started the dive I didn't notice it until after I had dropped my fish — too many things to think about! The destroyers must have been about 1,000 to 1,200yd from the battleship. It was quite tricky having to manoeuvre between two destroyers to get inside the screen and have a clear run for the torpedo. It then left very little time to adjust everything and drop the fish within the necessary criteria for a good run, namely — height 50 to 120ft above water — wings level — nose not down and not much up — aim off for the ship's speed at one's dropping range which had to be 800 to 1,000yd with the aircraft speed around 80kt. The torpedo sight on the Stringbag was two horizontal rows of light bulbs either side of the fuselage ahead of the pilot's cockpit.

You had to estimate the target speed and set it so that the correct bulb lit up. I estimated 30kt for the *Scharnhorst*. Of course we had never carried out practice attacks on big ships at that speed — most of ours didn't do more than 20 to 24kt.

'Anyway, after dropping the fish I did a violent starboard turn and went like hell at zero feet. I found this to be a mistake though, as all the shots being fired at me ricocheted off the sea all round the aircraft. I was just able to see my torpedo pass through the kick of the wake as *Scharnhorst* altered course — a miss just astern.

'I got away to the east and circled at about 1,000ft until two other aircraft joined me. We couldn't wait too long because of the fuel situation. Lt Smith gave me a course to steer and after four hours forty-five minutes flying we landed at RAF Sumburgh in the South Shetlands to refuel. We took-off again at 18.25 and landed at Hatston at 19.35. Four out of six got back and we never heard anything about the other two.'

In the spring of 1941 the *Bismarck* completed her sea trials and put to sea. On 20 May she was seen with the heavy cruiser *Prinz Eugen* and defending destroyers going through the Channel between the Danish islands leading from the Baltic to the Kateggat and Skagerrak. The next day RAF recce aircraft found them steaming towards Bergen, but a bombing raid was unsuccessful because of bad weather along the Norwegian coast. Next day the weather was even worse but a Maryland target-towing twin-engined aircraft took off from Hatston with a volunteer crew of pilot Lt Noel Goddard, observer Cdr G. A. Rotherham and TAG Milne. When they got to Bergen through abysmal weather they found the enemy had gone. Knowing that *Bismarck* was now at sea, Vice-Adm Sir John Tovey put to sea in *King George V* and with the only carrier available, *Victorious*. Now, *Victorious* had not been commissioned or worked up and, in fact, had been about to make a run to Malta with a load of Hurricanes. Consequently, her only aircraft were nine Swordfish of 825 Squadron and six Fulmars of 800Z Squadron, neither unit being up to strength or trained in the art of attacking large warships.

The British cruisers *Norfolk* and *Suffolk* found *Bismarck* on 23 May between Iceland and Greenland. *Norfolk* used her Walrus to shadow, but lost her again 48 hours later — and during that time the *Bismarck* and *Prinz Eugen* had engaged the *Hood* and *Prince of Wales* with tragic results: *Hood* had received direct hits and blown up with only three survivors from a ship's company of 1,422.

The C-in-C meanwhile was steaming at 27kt after the *Bismarck* but still had 300 miles to go, and Force H, with *Ark Royal*, was coming up from Gibraltar, but it too needed more time. It was essential to slow the *Bismarck* down so that it could be brought to action. Therefore, during the afternoon of 24 May, *Victorious* was detached from the main force with an escort to mount a strike against *Bismarck*. Subsequently a striking force of nine Swordfish led by Lt-Cdr E. Esmonde took off just after 22.00hrs — in the northern latitude sunset was not until after midnight. The

GREENLAND

Ice edge

Denmark Strait

Arctic Circle

MAY 23 8·32 pm
Cruisers Norfolk and
Suffolk sight and
shadow the
enemy

ICELAND

NORWAY

MAY 24 6·37 am
Hood sinks

MAY 22 6·30 pm
A Fleet Air Arm
Maryland reports
departure of Bismarck

Bergen

MAY 24 6·40 pm
Prince of Wales in action

MAY 24 11·30 pm
Fleet Air Arm Swordfish from
Victorious sight Bismarck

MAY 25 12·20 am
Swordfish attack Bismarck - one
hit reduces her speed

MAY 25 3·00 am
Bismarck shakes off
pursuers in poor visibility

MAY 26 10·30 am
Bismarck re-sighted by Catalina
of Coastal Command

MAY 26 11·15 am
Swordfish of Fleet Air
Arm from Ark Royal shadow
Bismarck

MAY 26 8·53 pm
Swordfish torpedo bombers from Ark
Royal cripple Bismarck

EIRE

GREAT
BRITAIN

Brest

FRANCE

MAY 27 11·01 am
Bismarck sunk by gunfire of the Fleet

Bay
of Biscay

NORTH

ATLANTIC

OCEAN

SPAIN

Right:
**The chase and destruction
of the *Bismarck*.**

weather was showery, with fresh winds and squalls, but visibility remained good. An ASV contact was made at 16 miles range and *Bismarck* was sighted shortly afterwards. Esmonde broke cloud cover only to find himself six miles away; the element of surprise was now gone and the flak started. It was so accurate that Esmonde's aircraft was hit while still four miles away, but he pressed on, leading his sub-flight right through the barrage and, when he was hit on the aileron, he decided to drop his fish on the port bow. Lt H. C. M. Pollard, leading one of the other sub-flights, attacked from the other side, while Lt P. D. Gick, leading the remaining sub-flight, was not happy with his approach and led the flight away to get a better run in. The TAGs vented their feelings by shooting up the *Bismarck's* gun positions and superstructure. At the end of the attack it appeared that one torpedo hit had been made: it was possibly enough to slow the ship down. All the aircraft returned safely through dreadful weather, and landed on a flight deck rising and falling 30ft. After one Swordfish had landed a huge wave swept over it, filling the cockpits with seawater — the pilot remarked afterwards that 'It was alright, the bottom of the fuselage had been shot away by the *Bismarck's* gunfire, so it soon drained.'

Meanwhile, the *Prinz Eugen* had broken away from *Bismarck* and proceeded at speed for Brest. On the next day, the 25th, the weather was worse, but a search was encouraged; this resulted in the loss of two Swordfish. One crew landed in the sea and was picked up by a trawler, but the other crew had an experience worthy of a book.

On the morning of 26 May a RAF Catalina sighted *Bismarck*, only to be driven off by gunfire. However, a Swordfish from the approaching *Ark Royal* shadowed the battleship until a strike could be laid on. In gale force winds and pouring rain, 14 Swordfish, armed with torpedoes, took-off from *Ark Royal* to attack the *Bismarck*. Flying through cloud they saw a grey shape in the water and in the appalling conditions mistook it for the *Bismarck* — in fact it was the *Sheffield*. Fortunately the 11 torpedoes launched at her all missed. A second strike was raised, with 15 Swordfish from 810, 818 and 820 Squadrons, and they made their attack under intense gunfire, achieving two hits: one was on the armoured belt, and the other, launched by 'Dilly' Dangerfield, hit the *Bismarck's* aft section, damaging propellers and jamming her rudders. Throughout the night she was snapped at by destroyers and in the morning, 27 May, another strike was laid on by *Ark Royal*. Capt T. Shaw was in at the end:

'The CO of 818 led 12 of us to torpedo the *Bismarck* but when we arrived it was not allowed because of the proximity of HM ships. The squadron passed half a mile astern of *Bismarck* at 1,000ft and as we watched she rolled over and sank. When we got back to *Ark Royal* the flight deck was moving through 65ft but we only had one undercarriage collapse — and that was because he had not jettisoned his torpedo. Shortly after that a Junkers 88 joined the circuit, but eventually he gave up, jettisoned his bombs and flew away.'

Left:
One of the Swordfish that made a torpedo strike against the *Bismarck* returns to *Ark Royal*.
IWM (A4100)

Below:
Swordfish K8376 '2Q' of 833 Squadron over Jamaica in October 1941. 'Queenie' was reputed to have made the torpedo strike that hit and crippled the *Bismarck*.
Lt-Cdr M. B. W. Howell

The other great action involving Swordfish and enemy capital ships was the magnificent action by six aircraft of 825 Squadron led by Lt-Cdr E. Esmonde against the might of the German Navy and the Luftwaffe. On 12 February 1942, Esmonde's aircraft attacked the battlecruisers *Scharnhorst* and *Gneisenau* and the cruiser *Prinz Eugen* as they headed out of the English Channel towards the North Sea. Without a fighter escort, the Swordfish gallantly pressed on into a powerful Luftwaffe fighter screen and flak barrage in an attempt to at least slow down one of the three warships, but they were unable to achieve a hit with any of their torpedoes. This story has been told so many times that readers must be well aware of the fact that there were only five survivors from the attacking force, and only one of them was not wounded. As a tribute to those brave men, let us at least put in the Roll of Honour:

W5984	Lt-Cdr E. Esmonde/ Lt W. H. Williams/ Leading Airman W. J. Clinton
W5983	Sub-Lt B. Rose/Sub-Lt E. Lee/ Leading Airman Johnson
W5907	Sub-Lt C. Kingsmill/ Sub-Lt R. M. Samples/ Leading Airman D. A. Bunce
W4523	Lt Thompson/ Sub-Lt Parkinson/ **Leading Airman E. Topping**
W5985	Sub-Lt Wood/ Sub-Lt Fuller-Wright/ Leading Airman Wheeler
W5978	Sub-Lt P. Bligh/ Sub-Lt W. Beynon/ Leading Airman Smith

The *London Gazette* announced that the King had awarded Esmonde the Victoria Cross, with the following citation:

'Lieutenant-Commander Esmonde knew well that his enterprise was desperate. Soon after noon he and his squadron of Swordfish set course for the enemy and after 10 minutes flight were attacked by a strong force of enemy fighters. Touch was lost with his fighter escort and in the action which followed all his aircraft were damaged. He flew on cool and resolute, serenely challenging hopeless odds, to encounter the deadly fire of the battlecruisers and their escorts which shattered the port wing of his aircraft.

'Undismayed, he led his squadron on, straight through this inferno of fire, in steady flight towards their target. Almost at once he was shot down, but his squadron went on to launch a gallant attack . . . from which not one of them returned.

'His high courage and splendid resolution will live in the traditions of the Royal Navy and remain for many generations a fine and stirring memory.'

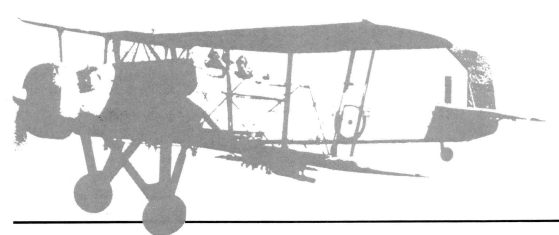

'THOSE IN WHOSE WORK THEY TRUST'

The title to this chapter of the book is taken from a prayer which the Fleet Air Arm used; it goes something like this: 'Almighty God, who makest the clouds Thy chariot and who walkest upon the wings of the wind, we commend to Thy fatherly protection all who ride the skies in the service of the fleet, and those in whose work they trust'.

When the Air Ministry, in its wisdom, handed over the control of aircraft flying under naval establishments or aircraft carriers to the Admiralty on 24 May 1939, it created another problem. The Navy's chief difficulty was that although it had plenty of pilots, observers and telegraphist air gunners, it had no maintenance ratings trained to service the aircraft. The problem was overcome only by the Air Ministry allowing a certain number of volunteers from the RAF to transfer to the Navy, and lending some 1,500 senior air artificers, fitters and mechanics to provide a nucleus of experience to the new organisation. At the same time the Navy began training its own body of maintenance ratings so that eventually the RAF tradesmen could return to their own service. Many of the RAF men retained their own uniform and mixed RAF and Royal Navy uniforms could be seen on many flight decks until well into the war.

The Navy had four categories of air fitter and air mechanic during the war.

The air fitters (A) were skilled tradesmen who had been in the engineering industry before joining up. They were accepted on passing a trade test and wore fore and aft rig — jacket and peak cap. They were the general assembly workers responsible for airframes and rigging, and were trained in sheet metal work, joinery and welding. The engine

mechanics (E) and machine operatives did not need to have had previous experience as every attempt was made by the Navy to put the right man in the right job. The electricians (L) looked after all the complicated wiring in the aircraft and other items such as the camera gun. The armourers, or ordnance men, (O) were responsible for all the armament and bombing equipment.

Radio mechanics were trained to look after all the telecommunications equipment in aircraft, a job that the Wrens, too, quickly learnt to do; in fact, the Navy began to train Wrens for the other trades as well. The training at trade school usually ran to about six months, after which the fitters and mechanics had to qualify at a Naval air station as competent to give a certificate of airworthiness to aircraft. After that they could serve ashore or afloat on a carrier.

In general, the usual procedure when flying from carriers at sea began when the pipe for ranging aircraft was sounded over the ship's Tannoy system and the first machines were brought up to the flight deck on the lift, with the wings still folded. The 'pin-party' of seamen pushed them into position on the flight deck and the maintenance crews spread the wings. Aircrew then climbed into their cockpits with the air mechanics helping them into their harnesses. Engines were started and the Petty Officer in charge of the flight would report all correct to the Deck Officer, who gave the signal to the Commander (Flying). This officer, known as 'Wings', would be looking down on the flight deck from his own position on the island and was in close contact with the Captain. Next, the ship turned into wind, and the Deck Officer brought the leading aircraft into position for the take-off by signalling to the pilot with a pair of small coloured flags. As soon as it had taxied into position, the 'stop' signal was given and the ratings handling the chocks placed them against the wheels to stop the aircraft from moving. When ready, ie into wind, the Commander (Flying) showed a green flag: this was the executive signal for flying off. The Deck Officer then signalled 'chocks away', the ratings removed the chocks and the aircraft would take-off. This procedure went on day or night, in all weathers.

On returning to the ship, the squadron or flight would go to a waiting position, usually about a mile astern, to

await the landing on order. The squadron distinguishing flag would then be shown at the No 1 port signal boom. The first sub-flight closed the ship and circled prior to lowering the hook. When the Commander (Flying) was ready he ordered the affirmative flag, a white cross on a red background, to be hoisted at No 2 port boom. From then on the pilot was under the orders of the Deck Landing Officer, who had to bring the aircraft in at the right height and speed over the round-down, the aft end of the flight deck. When he received the signal to land-on, the pilot would make a straight-in approach using plenty of engine power, nose well up, the aircraft virtually hanging on its prop as it sank

Top:
Engine already running, this Swordfish with wings folded is brought up from the depths of the ship with a combined RAF/Naval team.

Above:
This superb picture captures the halcyon days of a bygone era as a Swordfish is brought up by the lift to the flight deck of *Argus* for another day of deck landing training. *Fox Photos*

steadily towards the flight deck. Once over the round-down the signal was given by the Deck Landing Officer to 'cut' the engine so the hook should (theoretically) catch the first wire and bring the aircraft to a halt. Ratings would rush out to release the hook, the safety barrier was lowered and the aircraft taxied forward; then the barrier had to be raised again for the next aircraft. On its coming to a halt, the 'pin-party' pounced on the Swordfish, folded its wings and pushed it ready to be struck down, to the hangar where it would be parked ready for the squadron maintenance ratings.

It is perhaps fitting that the work of the Flight Deck Party is recorded by one so qualified — Ern Crimp:

The Aircraft Handler

They said, here's a job to keep you hale and hearty
I found myself as one of the Flight Deck Party —
Pushing aircraft around on a carrier's deck
And in general sticking out my ruddy neck,
Lying flat on the deck holding on to the chocks
Above me in slipstream the aircraft trembles and rocks,
With your wits all about you, you need to look out
For with all the noise, lost is my warning shout
You're very aware of that flashing airscrew
And all the damage that it could do,
'Away chocks' comes the signal, you then wrench them clear
As in all directions your eyes frantically peer,
To the edge of the deck you then run so fast
The aircraft takes off with a strong engine blast —
For a while there's a calm just meant to deceive
As the pipe then is made, 'Stand by to receive . . .'
Just when you thought that all danger had gone
Your job's now unhooking as they now land on!
Standing there on the deck as the aircraft swoop in
Is calculated to make your blood run thin . . .
To catch that steel hook on arrester wires
They slam to the deck with a scream from the tyres.

It's true that this job keeps you so hale and hearty
Though I have my doubts if this is a 'party'!
I was told it was all a part of the charm
Of being a sailor in the Fleet Air Arm —
We now push them on to the lift, strike them down
I believe we are slow . . . by our PO's heavy frown,
Then more aircraft come up and we all spread the wings
In fact we are doing remarkable things!
We run out of patience . . . We're getting 'Two blocks'
As we find we are lying back down with our chocks,
Then just to see if we can stand the strain
We fly off our aircraft all over again!
It seems as well as being hale and hearty
A sense of humour is needed in the Flight Deck Party . . .

Lying here at the wheel a nursing my chocks
I think of gentle sea that is wet on the rocks
Of gentle surf breaking so fine on the sand,
Peacetime seaside visits that really were grand
Of Reginald Dixon's organ at Blackpool Tower . . .
Or that Welsh rocky coast that they call the Gower,
Of Dartmoor, China clay pits of white . . .
Of cosily sleeping in a real bed at night
But on this flight deck a rolling away on the sea
All this is just but a dream now for me.

Ern Crimp

Top:
A prewar shot of Swordfish K5965. This machine joined 'A' Flight at Gosport in July 1936 before returning to Fairey in January 1941 for trials work.

Above:
'Stop me and buy one'. These naval ratings are removing equipment from the vehicle to fit to Swordfish at Crail.
Lt-Cdr R. E. F. Kerrison

Left:
RAF and Naval groundcrews with 820 Squadron Swordfish which have flown ashore to Dekheila from *Ark Royal* in April 1940. *Cdr R. N. Everett*

Top:
While one rating works on the rigging, two others chat over the tailplane of K8867 'G3P' which belonged to 812 Squadron. At that time 812 was embarked in *Glorious*, but 'G3P' is seen here at Dekheila near Alexandria.
Cdr R. N. Everett

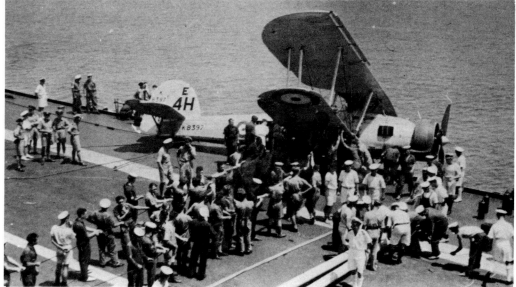

Centre right:
It is September 1939 and Lt-Cdr Eckersley-Maslin almost goes overboard as he lands K8397 'E4H' aboard *Eagle*. Ropes have been secured to hold the aircraft and the deck handling parties take up the strain.
E. B. Mackenzie

Bottom right:
'E4H' is saved from a wet grave as a jury rig lifts it clear of the side.
E. B. Mackenzie

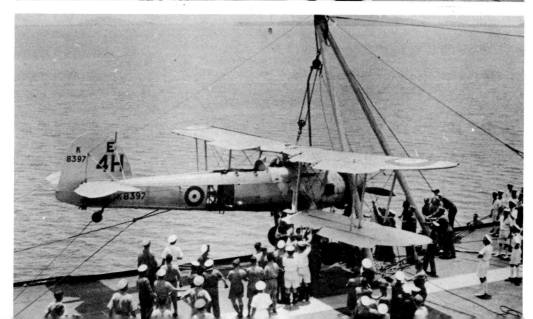

Top:
Deck crews go into action as a Swordfish crashes on to the flight deck of *Ark Royal* and bursts into flames.
Lt-Cdr M. B. W. Howell

Centre right:
Deck handlers try to save a Sea Hurricane from a watery grave as a Swordfish is waved away from *Argus*.
R. Fitzsimmonds

Bottom right:
Flying on *Ark Royal* is being held up as the engine mechanic tries to fix a problem and the crew gently tap their feet.
Cdr R. N. Everett

Top:
**A typical deck scene as a
tin-hatted deck party push a
Swordfish back off the lift.**
IWM (A16652)

Above:
**Rain-soaked ratings work
on a Swordfish of 768
Squadron as Petty Officers
Syd Hill and George Back
pop round to check up on
them in the Station
Armoury combination —
this shot was taken on
15 October 1944.** *J. Hagg*

Right:
**Ratings remove all reusable
items from this Swordfish of
813 Squadron which
crashed at Bone in North
Africa.** *Donoghue*

Left:
Removing the remains to the scrapyard. *Donoghue*

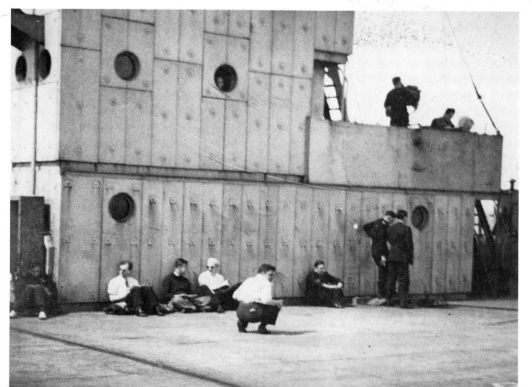

Above:
A nice one for the album — the flight deck crews of 'Easy Flight' of 836 Squadron aboard *Acastra* in 1944. *J. Taylor*

Left:
Flight deck crews idle in the sun as they await the return of 'their' aircraft.

Top right:
'Whatever next! Women working on aircraft — unthinkable, you won't get *me* flying in anything they've worked on, so there! Why, they'll want to be pilots next — where's me pink gin?' Wren radio mechanics working on a Swordfish. *IWM (A19132)*

Centre right:
A Wren works on a Swordfish that has been flying for six years and now needs a good overhaul. *IWM (A22058)*

Right:
Naval airmen bombing-up a Swordfish with 250lb bombs before taking off on another sortie. *IWM (A8221)*

94

STRINGBAGS IN THE MED

Italy's entry into the war on 10 June 1940 completely changed the balance of power in the Mediterranean. Italy, in the process of expanding its armed forces, had not scrimped on the size of its navy: the fleet consisted of six modern battleships, about 25 cruisers, at least 100 destroyers and large torpedo boats, and a similar number of submarines. Britain, protecting its oil supply routes, had bases at Gibraltar, Malta and Alexandria. Convoys with much-needed supplies from India, Australia, New Zealand and the Far East all passed through the Mediterranean on their way to the UK, and it was around these convoys that much of the Mediterranean action revolved. On 28 June 1940, Force H was formed with the task of covering any westward Italian thrusts and to bridge the gap left by the immobilisation of the French fleet. A few days before this, *Ark Royal* had arrived with three Swordfish Squadrons, 810, 818 and 820, with 30 aircraft between them, a much-needed addition to the Task Force.

The French fleet consisted of two new battlecruisers (*Dunkerque* and *Strasbourg*), two battleships, several light cruisers and some destroyers and submarines, all based at Mers-el-Kebir in Oran. It was Force H's unhappy task to ask the ships to join the Allies or suffer the consequences. The French declined and on 3 July Force H opened fire,

Swordfish from *Ark Royal* spotting for the guns, while five other Swordfish laid mines in the entrance to Mers-el Kebir harbour. Under the bombardment the old battleship *Bretagne* blew up and the *Dunkerque* was damaged and had to be beached, but the *Strasbourg* slipped out and made Bizerta. A strike by six Swordfish against her was met by heavy anti-aircraft fire and two Swordfish were lost. Six more Swordfish made a torpedo attack but, even though they achieved surprise, they did not make a hit due to poor tactics. Aerial reconnaissance showed that although the *Dunkerque* was aground, she was by no

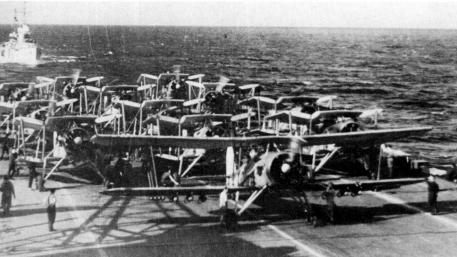

means done for, so on 6 July six Swordfish from 820 Squadron attacked her, achieving only one strike. The other squadron, 810, took 12 Swordfish and scored a number of hits. Meanwhile, *Hermes* had been shadowing the newly commissioned French battleship, the *Richelieu*. Six Swordfish from 814 Squadron aboard *Hermes* carried out a torpedo attack on 8 July and the one hit achieved put her out of action for over a year.

A few days before this, Swordfish of 813 Squadron had made a torpedo attack on enemy shipping in Tobruk harbour. Eight Swordfish dropped their torpedoes inside the harbour, getting hits on four ships, of which the destroyer *Zeffiro* and the liner *Liguria* were sunk and another destroyer and freighter damaged. The aircraft, although normally based on *Eagle*, were operating from the shore base at Sidi Barrani, and while there, Lt Collins hit and sank a submarine and then went over to machine gun the Tobruk airfield. The next few days proved to be quite hectic for *Eagle*, as TAG 'Ginger' Tyler's diary recorded:

'July 9 — I went off on a search at 4.45am. Some other units have joined up with the fleet. The Italian fleet has been sighted! We send off a torpedo striking force from 824 at 12.00. I went off again at about 12.30 to shadow the enemy fleet. We found them early in the afternoon; four battleships, ten cruisers and a large number of destroyers heading towards Taranto. Our own fleet

Top:
No 824 Squadron Swordfish ranged on the flight deck of *Eagle* on 9 July 1940 for an attack on the Italian fleet, the results of which were one destroyer and one submarine sunk, and one battleship and a cruiser damaged. *E. B. Mackenzie*

Above:
Swordfish of 813 and 824 Squadrons are ranged up for a bomb attack on Tripoli in 1940. The cruiser *Ajax* is behind. *E. B. Mackenzie*

Right:
A Swordfish from *Eagle* returns with its torpedo following an aborted strike on a group of Italian ships, because of bad weather. *E. B. Mackenzie*

was about two-thirds the size of theirs. The two fleets were converging and at about 15.30 the advance units went into action. The main battle started at about 16.00 and by 18.00 the enemy fleet were in full flight. We sent off another strike force and all the aircraft returned safely. There is no definite news about torpedo hits, nor of any enemy casualties. I came back to the ship after the beginning of the battle after having a grandstand view from 10,000ft. The enemy bombers started coming over about 17.30 and we had eight raids in two hours. Scores of bombs were dropped but there were no hits on any of our ships. All our ships were seaworthy after the battle and we had not lost a single casualty. When the enemy retired

we were continually bombed until sunset and after a very exciting day my tot will be the finest I've ever tasted.

'10 July — still at sea with the fleet. We had no air raids today, thank God. According to the news tonight the Italian fleet lost a destroyer and a submarine in yesterday's action. They had 29 dead and 69 wounded. We had no casualties at all. The Italians claim to have sunk this ship [*Eagle*] by bombs, and also a battleship. We sent off a torpedo force to attack the naval base at Port Augusta.'

This raid took place at dusk, when nine Swordfish of 813 Squadron arrived to find that the heavy ships had left and so they had to be content with sinking the

Above left:
A typical shore-based picture of Swordfish L9729 '4A' and P4137 '4K' of 820 Squadron ashore from *Ark Royal* at Dekheila in April 1940. *Cdr R. N. Everett*

Below:
A Swordfish of 820 Squadron taxies out at Dekheila in April 1940 with practice bombs under the wings. *Cdr R. N. Everett*

The Swordfish strike in Bomba Bay, 22 August 1940. The torpedoing of the depot ship and second submarine also resulted in the destruction of the destroyer.

B
O
M
B
A

B
A
Y

Submarine

CAPT PATCH
LT WELLHAM
LT CHEESMAN

Depot Ship
Submarine
Destroyer

Above:
The effects of camouflage are shown to good purpose as a Swordfish taxies past a camouflaged hangar.

Below:
This Swordfish, V4697, had taken part in the raid on Diego Suarez, and is seen here at Fayid in Egypt in December 1942 after being refurbished. *Howard Levy*

Below right:
Swordfish W5970 of 815 Squadron unfortunately nosed over in soft ground when the pilot landed to pick up the crew of an Albacore. Flying from Cyprus, 815 Squadron had made strikes against Vichy shipping in Syria.

destroyer *Leone Pancaldo* and damaging a fleet oiler. They brought the unused torpedoes back. The next day the Italians made 15 air attacks but again scored no hits.

During a rest-up, 824 Squadron moved up to Sidi Barrani and attacked shipping in Tobruk harbour, sinking the destroyers *Ostro* and *Nembo* in a moonlight torpedo strike. Many of the Swordfish sustained damage in this attack and Lt Brown being wounded and Petty Officer Wynn dying from his wounds the following day.

At the other end of the Mediterranean, nine Swordfish from *Ark Royal*, led by Lt-Cdr G. B. Hodgkinson, took off on 2 August to attack the airfield at Elmos. A mixed force from 810 and 820 Squadrons, they wrecked four hangars,

set buildings on fire and destroyed four aircraft on the ground. The Swordfish got away by flying along a country road — waving to the locals as they went. Early in September, 810 Squadron went back to Elmos in the early hours of the morning to carry out Operations 'Smash' (1 September) and 'Grab' (2 September), with no casualties.

In August, Swordfish from *Eagle* spotted for the bombardment of Bardia and then went ashore as *Eagle* moved into Alexandria harbour. A request for torpedo-carrying aircraft to help sort out some enemy shipping off the Libyan coast led to three Swordfish from 813 Squadron carrying out a number of anti-submarine patrols. On 21 August a RAF Blenheim spotted a submarine depot ship lying in Bomba Bay and a

Left:
Swordfish of 813 Squadron 'X' Flight based at the North Front, Gibraltar. The squadron's role was to detect U-boats passing through the Straits, with newly installed ASV.
Donoghue

Below:
Sub-Lt Donoghue flying V4615 '4A' of 813 Squadron near the Rock in 1943.
Donoghue

Bottom:
No 813 Squadron on daylight formation practice. Its later role was to disturb the nocturnal habits of U-boats — many hours were spent carrying out anti-submarine patrols, especially at night. *Donoghue*

submarine coming in from seaward. Early next morning Capt Patch RM, arrived to take over the flight and moved them up to Sidi Barrani. Armed with a torpedo each, the three Swordfish flew out to sea for about 50 miles before turning to make their run-in. Flying low over the sea they picked out the enemy vessels from about four miles away, the submarine opening fire when they got in range. Capt Patch, with observer Midshipman C. J. Woodley, faked a couple of passes and dropped his torpedo from 300yd, and a strike amidships caused the submarine to blow up in a spectacular explosion. The Swordfish on Patch's port side, flown by Lt J. W. G. Wellham with Petty Officer A. H. Marsh as his observer, flew on towards the other ships, which they quickly identified as the depot ship, another submarine and a destroyer. Lt N. A. F. Cheesman, with Sub-Lt F. Stovin-Bradford as observer, made his attack from landward to coincide with that of Wellham. Lt Cheesman's torpedo hit the submarine a few seconds before Lt Wellham's hit the depot ship just below the bridge. Flying out to sea, the Swordfish crews heard a terrific explosion and on looking back saw the three enemy vessels sinking from sight in a cloud of steam and smoke. Three old Stringbags had sunk four enemy ships with three torpedoes in as many minutes. All the crews were decorated with Patch getting the DSO.

In September the fleet had a welcome addition in the form of *Illustrious* with Swordfish of 815 and 819 Squadrons and Fulmars of 806. Meanwhile *Eagle*

Right:
This Swordfish was a replacement machine for Sub-Lt Donoghue, and is seen here on the lighters as it is brought ashore.
Donoghue

Below:
Sub-Lt Donoghue in front of Swordfish W5903 '5G' of 824 Squadron, also at Gib in 1943. *Donoghue*

had re-embarked her aircraft and on 4 September they attacked Rhodes. 'Ginger' Tyler went along on this one: 'Six aircraft from 824 and seven from 813 took part in this operation. The attack on Maritza was to coincide with *Illustrious's* attack on the seaplane base at Calato. Unhappily, our squadrons flew up the eastern coast of Rhodes and we could see *Illustrious's* aircraft attacking their target when we still had some way to go before we turned in over the hills to get at Maritza. Presumably the fighters at our target were alerted by the other attack and were waiting for us as we went in. Our two squadrons turned in and dived down into a bowl-like depression which held the aerodrome. With 813 leading we dived down, every gun in the place opening up on us. Soon the whole area was enveloped in bomb bursts as our pilots found their targets. As we pulled out of the dive to get out to sea we were pounced on by a number of Fiat CR42 fighters. I was not aware of any of our aircraft being shot down as I was too busy with my own business. Anyhow, the first wave was over and 824 went in to deliver their own load to add to the misery of the defenders. And so, out to sea we went, flying very low, back to the ship which was off the southeast coast of Crete, after a flight of over four hours. All 824 Squadron aircraft returned safely but sadly four of 813 failed to return.'

On 17 September, 15 Swordfish from *Illustrious* sank two Italian destroyers in Benghazi harbour and damaged a number of other ships. Then, 16 days after Taranto, Force H encountered the Italian fleet consisting of two battleships, six cruisers and 16 destroyers. Lt-Cdr M. Johnstone led off 11 Swordfish, all with torpedoes, but few hits were made. A second strike an hour later led by Lt-Cdr J. A. Stewart-Moore fared no better. To round off 1940, Swordfish from *Illustrious* bombed airfields in the Dodecanese and Aegean, the airfield at Rhodes and a convoy off Sfax. In a night attack by six Swordfish, two large Italian merchant ships were sunk by torpedoes.

At 05.55hrs on 2 February 1941, eight Swordfish of 810 Squadron from *Ark Royal* set out to torpedo the dam at Tirso in Sardinia. Strong gusty conditions forced one aircraft to return after getting separated, two had to jettison their torpedoes when the aircraft iced up, and Lt O'Sullivan was shot down on the approach. The other four Swordfish managed to release their torpedoes against the dam, but with no apparent effect. Fourteen Swordfish left *Ark Royal* to bomb the Azienda oil refinery and although 11 bombed there was no noticeable results. Three other Swordfish were sent out to spot for the bombardment of Genoa and four others mined the entrance to Spezia harbour. The only loss was one aircraft that got tangled in a balloon cable.

With the object of preventing the Italian fleet from entering the Aegean, 815 Squadron with six Swordfish were moved to Maleme under Lt-Cdr J. de F. Jago. Early in March the squadron moved to Eleusis near Athens and operated from there and a secret advanced base at Paramythia in the

Left, top to bottom:
**Air attacks on *Ark Royal* and her convoy
going through to Malta.**
Lt-Cdr M. B. W. Howell

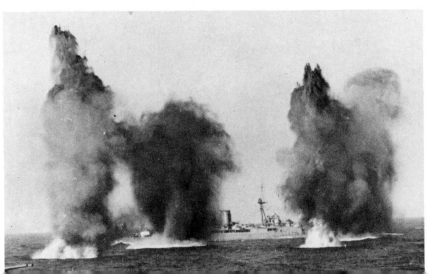

Albanian mountains. The CO and his observer, Lt Caldecott-Smith, were lost on the first operation and Lt F. M. A. Torrens-Spence took command. Seven sorties were mounted against Durazzo and when the Italians started to send in convoys the Swordfish followed, claiming three hits in a single night. Some 12 operations were mounted against Valona, resulting in five torpedo hits and two probables; during the final raid Lt Torrens-Spence torpedoed an ammunition ship in Valona harbour. Under pressure from the advancing Germans, however, 815 pulled back to Eleusis and finally evacuated, with the last two Swordfish getting airborne and away as the first Messerschmitts came into attack. During the five weeks that they had operated in the area, 815 Squadron had sunk five enemy ships, damaged five others and caused other damage out of proportion to the tiny force.

Also in 1941, German activities in Iraq had been a thorn in the side of the British Government for some time and Cdr N. Martin RN (Retd) recalls one intervention:

'I was CO of 814 Squadron from March 1941 until the old *Hermes* was sunk off Ceylon on 9 April 1942. We spent our time endlessly patrolling between the Seychelles and Colombo/Trincomalee. In June 1941 we were suddenly ordered into the Persian Gulf to operate 814 Squadron in support of the Army who were quelling Raschid Ali's invasion of Iraq. With temperatures of 100°F to 120°F, no wind, no catapult in *Hermes*, and *Hermes's* speed about 20kt different to our Swordfish, we had to operate from ashore as we would never have got off the deck with full petrol and bomb load. We were ordered to bomb and destroy the railway bridge at Samawa up the Euphrates. Operating out of Shaibah, a RAF station, we duly took off

Above:
A Swordfish seen immediately after taking off from Ark Royal.
Lt-Cdr M. B. W. Howell

Below:
Swordfish landing and taking off from Ark Royal in the Mediterranean.

and all 12 of us missed hitting the bridge. On the way back Sub-Lt Pooley blew his engine and force-landed in the desert. Lt James Dundas, his flight leader, landed with great skill alongside him, picked up the crew and with six people in the Swordfish returned to Shaibah. Dundas was awarded a DSC.

'There is however a sequel to the story. On returning to *Hermes* out in the Gulf I dejectedly reported to the Captain that we had failed. He roared with laughter and said that after we'd taken off to bomb the bridge he'd received a signal from the C-in-C and asked us not to! He couldn't get through to us in the air but heard from Shaibah that we'd missed — so he sent a signal to C-in-C saying that we had made a determined show of force near the bridge but that no attempt had been made to hit it.'

One squadron that had been flying regularly from *Ark Royal* and *Argus*, 812, found itself based for a time at Gibraltar. Using Swordfish fitted with ASV, the aircraft operated at night in the Straits, damaging five U-boats in three weeks. *U451* was sunk by 812 Squadron on the night of 21/22 December 1941, thus indicating the valuable aid that ASV became.

By now the Swordfish were becoming a bit dated for ops from fleet carriers and their role was increasingly taken over by newer types. However, the success of ASV night patrols by 812 Squadron meant that these operations should continue and 813 Squadron took them on for a time. To cover a wider area a sub-flight was located at Blida and another at Bone. On the night of 14 December 1942, 813 Squadron carried out what well may have been the last Swordfish torpedo operation of the war.

Above:
The flight deck of *Ark Royal* becomes a hive of activity as the Swordfish start their engines. *Cdr R. N. Everett*

Below:
A Swordfish on the flight deck of *Ark Royal* causes a hiccup in the programme as everyone offers advice. *Cdr R. N. Everett*

According to the squadron diary, the event went something like this. All personnel were shaken out at 02.00hrs, and a strike of seven air- craft was airborne at 03.40hrs for a 'blitz' on Bizerta Lake. The attack force was in two waves, the first wave consisting of:

4A	Lt Hankey/Lt Hutchinson/PO(A) Hensman	18in Duplex torpedo
4B	Sub-Lt Allison/Sub-Lt White/LA Tidd	18in Duplex torpedo
4C	Sub-Lt Hill/Sub-Lt Abel/LA Parry	18in Duplex torpedo
4F	Sub-Lt Empson/Sub-Lt Pears/APO(A) McBride	Flares/two 250lb GP bombs

The second wave consisted of:

4K	Sub-Lt Heath/Lt Weatherall/PO(A) Goddard	Torpedo
4L	Sub-Lt Robinson/Sub-Lt Timberlake/LA Smith	Torpedo
4Q	Sub-Lt Baring/Sub-Lt Legood/LA Johnston	21 flares/two 250lb bombs

The plan was to attack two motor vessels reported anchored 1½ miles off the North Mole approximately 060° from Ferryville. Of the first wave, '4C' became detached during the outward flight and failed to locate the target. '4F' also got detached and arrived over the target late. '4A' and '4B' arrived at 2,000ft and proceeded to let down to 100ft and then '4A' attacked from around 50ft and dropped its torpedo at 700yd; a flash was seen, but it may have been gunfire. Meanwhile '4B', suffering ASV failure, stooged around waiting for the flares to drop — when these appeared the pilot dropped from around 30ft, aiming at a large motor vessel. '4F', the flare drop- per, bombed what was thought to be a W/T station, but no results were observed in the dark. Attacking by the light of flares, '4K' scored a hit 40sec after release, with a violent explosion and a column of smoke curling up to 2,000ft that could be seen from a distance of 70 miles. Unfortunately '4L' got too low, dipped his wheels in the water and quickly released his torpedo to stagger into the air, while '4Q' attacked the dock area with bombs, but did not observe any results. All the aircraft arrived safely back at Bone between 07.15hrs and 08.00hrs. The only observed opposition had been some rifle fire.

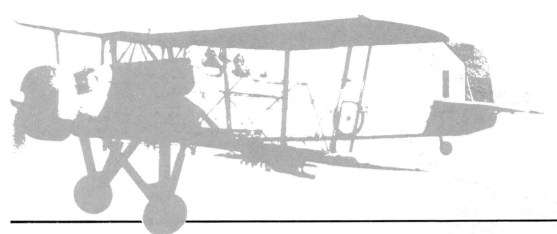

SWORDFISH AND ESCORT CARRIERS

In the summer of 1940, Germany overran Europe in a very short time, leaving Britain isolated and reliant on its merchant fleet, one of the biggest in the world, to ensure supplies of foodstuffs, raw materials and armaments. In order to protect this shipping, the ship convoy system was quickly introduced. One of the biggest problems in providing comprehensive cover for these convoys was the lack of aerial protection in the central Atlantic, where the shore-based aircraft of RAF Coastal Command could not reach, and it was this so-called 'gap' where the enemy made full use of its U-boats, which were kept informed by the very long-range Focke Wulf Fw200 Condor aircraft operating out of Bordeaux/Merignac. These four-engined aircraft would fly out into the Atlantic and report to the U-boat commanders when they detected convoys, and were not averse to making the odd attacks on individual ships themselves.

In an effort to take the advantage away from the enemy, the Admiralty converted a number of merchant ships to carry catapult-launched fighters. Five such conversions were made, and four of these saw service with convoys. The aircraft carried were usually Fulmars or Hurricanes; after being launched and making their attack, they either ditched near one of the ships in the convoy or flew ashore if within

range. These ships were replaced by the Catapult Armed Merchant (CAM) ships, whose only significant difference was that the pilots were provided by the RAF and that the ships still flew the Red Ensign. Some 35 CAM ships were introduced, and while they may not have knocked down many of the enemy, there was no denying the deterrent value of their aircraft. These ships sailed on 170 round trips with North Atlantic, Arctic and Gibraltar convoys, making eight operational launches that resulted in the destruction of six enemy aircraft and damage to three others. Twelve of the CAM ships were lost in action.

At the outbreak of war Germany had 57 U-boats, and by the end of 1942 this had risen to 417, with another 68 Italian vessels — by then the Germans were building U-boats faster than the Allies could destroy them. During World War 2 Axis U-boats sank, on average, 40 ships a month, in return losing 781 German and 85 Italian submarines sunk by all means.

The appalling convoy losses in the Atlantic and the limited success of the CAM ships caused the Admiralty to dig out some prewar plans to convert merchant ships into auxiliary aircraft carriers, which were later known as escort carriers, more closely reflecting the role they were to play. Appropriately, the first conversion was the

Below:
A Swordfish taking off from the camouflaged *Fencer*. 842 Squadron was embarked in *Fencer* when her Swordfish sank three U-boats in two days. *A. Rudd*

Bottom:
How close can you get? A Swordfish passes across the bows of *Smiter* as another is ranged for take-off. *Smiter* was not made operational until August 1945 and just missed the action.

captured German ship, the *Hannover*. She was fitted with a flush deck about 460ft long and had two arrester wires and a crash barrier. Renamed *Audacity*, she began operations in September 1941 and immediately proved the escort carrier concept by shooting down five Condors, damaging three others and driving off a ninth.

Only four other British-built escort carriers saw service because the Ministry of War Transport would not release good fast merchant ships for conversion, instead ordering American-built escort carriers. The four British-built carriers were named *Activity*, *Vindex*, *Campania* and *Nairana*, and they all entered service in early 1944, operating with considerable success in Arctic convoys. Between February and April 1944 *Activity* embarked 819 Squadron with Swordfish and Wildcats and then 833 Squadron until August, during which time the carrier took part in 14 Gibraltar convoys and one anti-submarine sweep. *Nairana* embarked 835 Squadron with Swordfish and Hurricanes from February to September 1944 and took part in 13 Gibraltar convoys and one anti-submarine sweep. Her Sea Hurricanes shot down two Junkers Ju290B aircraft in March 1944. *Vindex*, with the highly experienced 825 Squadron embarked, was at first chosen to work with the 6th Escort Group in the South West Approaches as part of a hunter/killer operation. The Swordfish made several attacks and on 15 March they shared in the destruction of *U653* with the sloops *Starling* and *Wild Goose* in a night attack. This success was followed up on 6 May when 825 Squadron shared *U765* with the American-built escorts, *Bligh*, *Bickerton* and *Aylmer*. *Vindex* then went on to Arctic convoys and continued her run of kills. On 24 August, 825's Swordfish shared in the destruction of *U344* and the following day sank *U354* by themselves. Swordfish of 825 Squadron were again in action on 2 September when

Above:
Swordfish LS231 'D', flown on to *Striker* by Sub-Lt J. C. H. Simpson on 1 September 1944, missed the wires and hit the barrier so hard the engine fell off!
Cdr J. H. Stenning

Left:
Another Swordfish, LS191 'A' of 842 Squadron, comes to grief on *Fencer*. *A. Rudd*

Above:
**Whoops — Sub-Lt
J. R. Harrison in NF116 'V'
makes a hard landing
aboard *Striker* on 26 March
1944.** *Cdr J. H. Stenning*

Centre right:
**Definitely not the way to
arrive — it upsets the
goofers! This scene is on
Fencer, 1943.** *A. Rudd*

Right:
**The moment is caught by
the camera lens: the
undercarriage of this
Swordfish collapses as it
lands aboard *Fencer*.**
A. Rudd

they again shared in the destruction of a submarine, this time *U394*. The fourth ship, the *Campania*, went on six Gibraltar convoys, embarking 12 Swordfish and four Wildcats of 813 Squadron between June and August 1944. If there had been any doubt in the minds of the people behind the escort carrier concept, they could surely dispel them as the results came in.

The use of fighters as part of an anti-submarine strike team, usually with Swordfish, was a complete success. As tactics developed it was found more and more that if a U-boat was found on the surface by a patrolling Swordfish it would stay and fight. As the Swordfish was relatively vulnerable to this sort of attack, it would then whistle up the fighters and a combined attack would take place: when the Swordfish made its attack with rockets, bombs or depth charges, the fighters would sweep in and strafe the U-boat, forcing the gunners to keep their heads down.

The American-built escort carriers were all diesel-powered and had wooden flight decks. They were known as CVEs, and the first so ordered, *Archer*, made only one brief operational trip in the summer of 1943 because she suffered continually from machinery defects. Also, the CVEs did not match up to Admiralty standards for fuel and fire protection, which was amply demonstrated on 15 November 1942 when *Avenger* was torpedoed by *U155* and sank after one hit; then in March 1943 *Dasher* blew up due to aviation fuel combustion. It was also found that the ships required frequent refits due to continuous harsh wartime treatment, for which the hull and propulsion systems had not been designed.

The second American CVE, *Avenger*, embarked three Swordfish and 12 Sea Hurricanes to join convoy PQ18 off Iceland on 9 September 1942. One of her Swordfish reported a U-boat sighting and shortly afterwards *U589* was sunk by escorting destroyers. *Biter* became the first escort carrier to make the North Atlantic run in April 1943, embarking Swordfish and Wildcats of 811 Squadron for all of the ship's 16 subsequent Gibraltar and trans-Atlantic convoys. It was on one of these Atlantic convoys that *Biter's* Swordfish shared in the destruction of *U203* with the destroyer *Pathfinder* and not long after-

wards the *U89* with the ex-US destroyer *Broadway* and the frigate *Lagan*. History was made in the early hours of 23 May 1943 when *U752* latched on to a convoy about 750 miles west of Ireland and proceeded to shadow it. Sub-Lt H. Horrocks, on an anti-submarine patrol in his Swordfish, spotted the U-boat and under cover of cloud managed to get within 300yd before firing rockets at it

— the first time that a rocket projectile had been fired operationally by any of the allied forces. One of the rockets — capable when fired at a range of 600yd of penetrating both the near and far plating of a submarine pressure hull — pierced the hull, causing considerable damage and so the submarine crew surfaced to fight it out. Horrocks then whistled up the Martlet fighters which

Above:
On 27 December 1943 Sub-Lt Pete Aked ballooned while landing LS245 'K' on *Striker* and collapsed the undercarriage.
Cdr J. H. Stenning

Right:
A U-boat being attacked by a Swordfish from *Fencer* during a return convoy from Russia in May 1944.
A. Rudd

Far right top:
The arctic conditions on the runs to Russia are legendary. Here deck parties sweep *Fencer's* flight deck in an effort to stay operational while on the way to Russia in May 1944. *A. Rudd*

Far right bottom:
No, *Fencer* is not sinking, but experiencing some of those Arctic conditions as she sails on a Russian convoy in 1944. *E. W. Tyler*

strafed the bridge and guns, killing the Captain and some of the crew. As the tanks flooded, *U752* sank, the first case of an escort carrier aircraft being solely responsible for the sinking of a U-boat. This was the last Fleet Air Arm success in the Atlantic until *U666* was sunk by Swordfish of 842 Squadron embarked in *Fencer* in February 1944.

July 1943 saw 818 and 824 Squadrons embarked in the ex-maintenance carrier *Unicorn* with 13 Swordfish and 10 Seafires. *Unicorn* then joined *Illustrious* to create a diversionary sweep to draw attention away from the Allied landings in Sicily.

There was a serious lack of Royal Naval carrier-borne capability in the Indian Ocean after the Japanese had sunk *Hermes* in April 1942, but no relief could be found until September 1943 when *Battler* arrived with 12 Swordfish and six Seafires of 834 Squadron on board. Adm Somerville, disenchanted with his close escort role, adopted the hunter/killer tactics and was rewarded on 12 March 1944 when a Swordfish sank an enemy supply ship and guided nearby ships on to another.

The first escort carrier to complete the round trip to Russia was *Chaser* during February/March 1944. Embarked were 11 Swordfish and 11 Wildcats of 816 Squadron, and these aircraft sank *U366* and *U973* and shared in the destruction of *U472*. On the Russian convoys it then became standard practice to have two escort carriers and in March/April 1944 these were *Tracker* and *Activity*. *Activity* had three Swordfish of 819 Squadron and seven Wildcats, while *Tracker* had 846 Squadron with 12 Avengers and seven Wildcats. During their tour, these squadrons shot down six shadowing aircraft, sank *U288*, shared in the destruction of *U355* and damaged three other U-boats. Swordfish continued to be embarked in escort carriers on Russian convoys and from spring 1944 until the end of the war only four merchant ships were sunk by the enemy out of 304 despatched, while the Germans lost seven U-boats during three convoys; in two days in May 1944, Swordfish of 842 Squadron in *Fencer* sank three U-boats the *U277*, *U674* and *U959*. By now the writing was on the wall and U-boats started operating in coastal waters, using the new schnorkel equipment. It was Swordfish from 842 Squadron which provided anti-submarine patrols for the first strike on *Tirpitz* on 3 April 1944 and supplied three Swordfish for similar duties from *Furious* for the second series of strikes.

Norway became the focal point of operations early in 1945, and during the night of 28 January Swordfish of 813 Squadron embarked in *Campania* made a rocket attack on three enemy trawlers illuminated by flares, sinking all three. Other strikes against the last German resistance in Norway was carried out by 14 Swordfish and six Wildcats of 835 Squadron.

'LILY'

Below:
Lt Jeffs flies over the floating airstrip known as 'Lily' in Lamlash harbour, Isle of Arran. *J. R. Jeffs*

During World War 2 there were many interesting and exciting inventions that were, in the long run, designed to either shorten the war or at least make it easier for the forces to conduct their operations. Two such inventions were Ronald Hamilton's 'Swiss Rolls' and 'Lily Ponds'.

The idea of operating vehicles along a floating road and aircraft from a floating airstrip was conceived by Mr Hamilton, a former Royal Navy Petty Officer of the Royal Naval Patrol Service, who saw both ideas built and tested. It was 1940 when he thought of using a flexible metal carpet that floated on the sea as a landing surface for aircraft. Helped by a mathematics housemaster at Eton, J. S. Herbert, Hamilton wanted to use the natural surface tension of water to hold the road or airstrip, which

he thought should be able to flex in every way with the flow of water and take shocks in the normal manner. To test his theory Hamilton borrowed a length of farm palings, rested it on the surface of a stream, covered it with tarpaulin and then rode across it on a motorbike at 50mph. His experiment at least proved one of his theories, that the faster the speed of crossing, the more rigid the surface. Laying such a flexible surface over the water and increasing the tension over 400,000 times allowed it to take very heavy loads: as an example, during the invasion landings at Normandy in 1944, laden lorries were driven across a pier of flexible canvas and wood that stretched from ship to shore and could support loads of 18-30 tons. This pier was codenamed 'Swiss Roll' after the manner in which the surface material could be rolled up.

With the airstrip, Hamilton believed that the solution lay in floating hundreds of six-sided buoyancy cans, 6ft wide and 30in deep, linked and clamped in a manner that allowed them to 'give' in waves or undulations while retaining a rigid surface that could take the weight of an aircraft. From above, the construction looked rather like a honeycomb until the surface was laid on top. The name 'Lily' came from the resemblance of the honeycomb to close masses of water lilies.

The full-scale development of these ideas was carried out by the Miscellaneous Weapons Development Branch of the Admiralty, which decided to test the practicality of operating aircraft

from a floating airstrip. The calm weather trials for 'Lily' were made in Lamlash Harbour in the Isle of Arran, far from prying eyes. A Swordfish was chosen to conduct the first trials and other types would follow if they were successful. Initially it was intended to conduct calm weather tests and then introduce waves, the latter getting larger as the tests progressed. Various naval officers, ratings, Admiralty observers, mechanics, photographer, batsmen, scientists and doctors (just in case) were on the strip for the tests. The pilot selected to carry out the flying trials was Lt Ray Jeffs RNVR, and he recorded his part in the proceedings:

'Before we started these trials I went over to Lamlash Harbour to have a look at "Lily" so that I'd have a fair idea of what was going to happen when I was flying from the strip. I was amazed to see how flexible the strip was — each little wave was accurately reproduced, and it didn't somehow seem possible that an aircraft of 9,000lb could operate safely. From the air the strip looked quite solid and its size, 520ft by 60ft, was anything up to a 100ft longer than the flight deck on MAC ships. I'd served in these ships on the Atlantic convoy route for just over 18 months.

'The strip, officials, observers and the aircraft were all ready. The trials began, and I for one held my breath as I approached to land on. The main difference between landing on the strip and on a carrier is that the approach is made so low over the water (the free-board was only 17in). The undulations can't be seen until the aircraft is quite close to the strip and even then

Top left:
The Swordfish catches the wire as Lt Jeffs lands on 'Lily'. *J. R. Jeffs*

Left:
Ratings release the wire from the hook of the Swordfish as others start to push it back. Note that the weight of the aircraft has caused the strip to sink slightly. *J. R. Jeffs*

they seem pretty small. In calm weather the landings and the hooking of the arrester wire are exactly the same as on a carrier — except of course, as the aircraft touches down there is a prolonged clanging from the cans! This can be heard above the engine noise. As the aircraft comes to rest its weight causes an indentation of about 10in.

'Taking-off is rather frightening at first — the effect of the groove caused by the aircraft's weight is like driving through deep sand when you are on the point of becoming bogged. The aircraft, which was fully loaded for its type, was fitted with rocket-assisted take-off gear and it is when this is fired that the aircraft jumps forward and slowly the groove gets shallower as the aircraft picks up speed. I had been landing on and flying off in winds down to seven knots. Here again is a big difference between "Lily" and the carrier. "Lily" is moored to a buoy and flying operations rely solely on the natural wind — a carrier can steam at any speed when operating aircraft, and so makes its own wind. On one occasion I nearly met with disaster and that was the last take-off. I was sure that both the aircraft and I were in for a ducking. There I was (as they say in the air force) with engine and rockets doing their utmost to get me airborne and the wire (caught up) was trying to hold me back. All was well though and I managed to pull the aircraft up, although I wished I had a pair of sculls at the time.'

Although the end of the war finished off any further trials, readers might like to consider the possibilities that exist for an updated model of 'Lily', with Harriers operating from forward concealed positions in conjunction with attack helicopters, or using it as a forward base hospital supplied by helicopters.

Top:
A MTB runs down the side of 'Lily' to create wave undulations, shown to good effect in this picture.
IWM (A30256)

Right:
Lt Jeffs 'just' airborne at the end of his take-off run. Note the RATO gear without which it might not have been possible to get a laden Swordfish off in that distance. *J. R. Jeffs*

MAC STRINGBAGS

The Merchant Aircraft Carriers — MAC ships — came along at an important time: the conversion and delivery of ships to escort carrier configuration was slow because construction took longer than had been anticipated. A more simple arrangement adopted was the conversion of grain ships or tankers, whereby a simple flight deck was constructed over the existing structure. Due to the layout, the grain ships were provided with a lift and space for four Swordfish, whereas the tankers had a longer flight deck and no lift. The beauty of these conversions was that the layout still allowed more than 80% of the original area to be used, thus making the ships dual-purpose, and altogether 13 tankers and six grain ships were converted. Although there is no doubt as to the contribution these ships made when augmenting the escort carriers, their work was boring and monotonous, and the following statistics give no real appreciation of the conditions under which the crews operated.

MAC ships sailed in 217 convoys and made 323 Atlantic crossings, for which some 4,447 days were spent at sea, of which 3,057 were in convoy. Flying took place on 1,183 of those days, and 114 Swordfish were lost or damaged beyond repair, the aircrews achieving 4,177 sorties in 9,016 flying hours; six pilots, five observers and eight TAGs were killed. Twelve attacks were made against U-boats, though none of them were sunk. It is, however, true to say that the introduction of MAC ships gave

the U-boats little opportunity to achieve any success against any convoy containing them. Three squadrons were set up to operate Swordfish from these ships, 836, 840 and 860 (the latter being a unit of the Royal Netherlands Navy), and by early 1944 they had 92 Swordfish on strength between them.

On 7 May 1943, Lt-Cdr Ransford W. Slater became the first pilot in history to land an aircraft on a merchant ship when he took Swordfish V4570 on to the converted *Empire MacAlpine*. He then carried out five further landings before ferrying Adm Boyd (the 5th Sea Lord), Capt Pugh and Lt O'Neil ashore to Machrihanish as the first passengers to fly off a MAC ship. Later that same day he returned with the squadron and carried out deck landing trials with complete success. Lt-Cdr Slater was late of 830 Squadron on Malta and had taken command of 836 Squadron in July 1942.

Top left:
Swordfish tea party? Not quite: the original 836 Squadron aircraft got lost while flying over Cuba and put down in a clear patch — hence the welcoming party at Quatros Cominos. In fact there was a large American air base about two minutes flying away which the crew had missed! *J. K. G. Taylor*

Top right:
Here two Swordfish are in the water and a third is also down, out of the picture. On 31 August 1942 a training flight of four aircraft took off for Skipness ranges in misty low cloud. Over Campbeltown conditions worsened, the CO pulled up slow and the two Swordfish behind stalled into the water. The third aircraft following was also hemmed in and attempted to land on the beach — but ended up in the water! The CO, Lt-Cdr R. W. Slater, made it back to Machrihanish.
J. K. G. Taylor

Centre right:
Photographs of 840 Squadron are hard to come by, but this is one. Nos 840, 836 and 860 Squadrons were MAC units. *D. Hall*

Right:
A Swordfish of 860 Squadron banks round past *Gadila,* **both being units of the Netherlands Naval Air Service.**
Royal Netherlands Navy

The *Empire MacAlpine* also sailed in a convoy of around 40 ships, but this was purely a propaganda trip and the first operational deployment was when she joined a large convoy in September 1943. This was none too soon. The few escort carriers available had been withdrawn to support the North African landings and U-boats had sunk more than two million tons of shipping. The first convoy with *Empire MacAlpine* included the combined ONS18 and ON202 which consisted of 66 merchant ships and 17 escorts. On the very first sortie the new outfit showed its true mettle and gave a foretaste of standards to come. On 21 September 1943, Sub-Lt R. A. Singleton took off with his observer, Acting Lt-Cdr J. Palmer, on Patrol 1. The occasion is best summed up in the words of the Senior Officer, Escort:

'*Empire MacAlpine*, having flown off an aircraft as soon as visibility permitted, suddenly found herself enshrouded in fog. Her aircraft made one of the most amazing landings I have ever heard of, getting on her tiny deck in absolutely dense fog.' In fact, Singleton landed with visibility down to 50yd, helped by the accuracy of the ship and aircraft radar. Patrols were carried out in all weather conditions and it was only the next day that Sub-Lt B. I. Barlow in HS381, with observer Sub-Lt J. Boyd, detected a U-boat on the surface. Sub-Lt P. T. Gifford took off in LS281 with his observer, Lt J. H. G. Tapscott, to join Barlow and they then made independent attacks with rockets and depth charges, but missed due to heavy return gunfire.

By October 1943 three more MAC ships had become operational and that month a Swordfish from *Rapana*

damaged a U-boat shadowing astern of convoy SC143. All 19 MAC ships were in service by May 1944 and as each ship neared completion a new flight of three or four Swordfish would be formed at Maydown in Northern Ireland, along with the required number of air and groundcrews. Each new flight was given a letter from 'A' Flight onwards and after working up would join its carrier in the Firth of Clyde. As an example, a tanker conversion would have three Swordfish, a Petty Officer in charge of four fitters, four riggers, three electricians (one specialising in radar), and two armourers (or AMOs — Air Mechanic Ordnance — as they are known in the Navy). Describing what it was like to join a MAC ship is Lt-Cdr John Godley, later Lord Kilbracken:

'On 23 October 1943 I was airborne out of Maydown on the grey and gusty morning, 10 seconds behind Phil Blakey and with Johnnie Gilbert just behind me. Quickly into formation with him, only 4ft separating our mainplanes. Turning short of Derry for the usual show-off fly-past of the Maydown con-

trol tower at zero feet with all the boys waving. Following the Irish coast, skirting the Mull of Kintyre, climbing over Arran for our Firth of Clyde rendezvous. And there, unmistakable on a straight southerly course, with her white wake streaming astern, was our seemingly brand-new parent vessel, *Acavus*, ready to receive us.

'First impression — Jesus, she's like a postcard! A signal from Phil and we plunge down in a dive, keeping formation as we make another ceremonial flypast at flight deck level. We break up on a signal from Phil and go into line astern as *Acavus* begins her turn into wind. As Phil begins his approach I can see the batsman on his port-side platform near the aftermost end of the flight deck. We would normally land three aircraft in less than a minute but as this is the first time for all of us, air and deck crews, I leave at least three minutes between Phil's landing and my own. I see Phil touch down safely and taxi forward, the safety barrier being raised behind him. Now it's my turn. "Come on ahead", signals the batsman. My airspeed is 65, I close the throttle slightly, ease back on the stick to lose five knots. "Bats" changes his signal: "A wee bit lower". Slightly close the throttle, forward with the stick, till he's again telling me to come on as I am. A last moment, "Come lower". I throttle back, then, at 15ft or so as I cross the stern, the mandatory crossed-bats signal commanding "Cut your engine". I do so and sink gently to a three-pointer, catching the first wire.

'Groundcrews race towards me from the safety nets to disengage my hook. I taxi smartly ahead of the barrier and switch off. Half-a-dozen crewmen race

towards me to manhandle my Stringbag alongside Phil's. The barrier already raised behind me, I see Johnnie's aircraft approaching. We clamber from our cockpits and head for the bridge as he lands.

'Prangs were fairly commonplace. And one more disadvantage of having no hangar soon showed itself. If, as a result of a quite minor accident such as the undercarriage collapsing, a Stringbag became difficult or impossible to manhandle forward and aft as necessary to allow aircraft to operate; it would often be pitched overboard without delay or ceremony. After one such prang in *Acavus* we were given more than the usual time to dispose of the carcass. We removed such useful parts as could be quickly extracted — the wireless, the clock, the bomb carriers, the radar set — and then announced on the loudspeakers that the Stringbag's corpse would be ditched over the side in half-an-hour; meantime all could help themselves. The whole ship's company descended on it like ants. When the allotted 30 minutes had elapsed, there was nothing left to throw overboard.

Above:
Dutch Navy 'Sugar One' Swordfish NE951 just after touch-down on the *Gadila*: note the Dutch triangle at the top of the rudder.
Royal Netherlands Navy

Below left:
Swordfish HS650 about to be pushed over the side of *Empire MacCabe*.
J. S. G. Mitchell

Below:
Another Swordfish about to end in a wet grave. Note the Mickey Mouse emblem.
J. K. G. Taylor

Top left:
A rear view as a Swordfish of 'Easy' Flight sets off on its take-off run from Acastra . . .

Top right:
. . . airborne over the numbers it continues on its way . . .

Centre right:
. . . leaving the flight deck — which doesn't look very big . . .

Right:
. . . and climb away safely.
All J. K. G. Taylor

The entire aircraft had been sawn and ripped apart for souvenirs and was distributed in small bits and pieces all over the ship.'

When U-boats started using the new schnorkel equipment it became more difficult to detect them, especially when they began to hug the coastlines. With this decline in activity it was decided it would be safe to use some of the MAC ships to ferry aircraft across the Atlantic on deck. James Mitchell was one of the merchant seamen aboard *Empire MacCabe*, one of the MAC ships involved.

'In early March we sailed for New York. On arrival we were boarded by a swarm of workmen who commenced drilling holes, in pairs, all over the flight deck. U bolts were then inserted with the bottom of the "U" uppermost. It was apparent that we were to carry a deck cargo. After loading our normal cargo of fuel oil, we shifted berth to a dry cargo-handling dock where we had loaded on to the flight deck a mixture of Vultee Vengeance and Lockheed Lightning aircraft, each swathed in a protective film of plastic. The astonishing dovetailing of 'plane into 'plane so that the maximum number would fit within a given area showed the planning which had gone into the whole operation. We could not now operate as a convoy escort, of course, but there was always the *MacMahon* or *Miranda*, or so we thought. We were astounded to see our two sister ships similarly encumbered. This was to be no ordinary convoy. In this we were right. A few days later more than 150 merchantmen were formed up in a massive armada to cross the Atlantic.'

In fact MAC ships ferried 212 aircraft over from New York during March/April in 11 voyages. Most of the cargoes were for the forthcoming invasion of Normandy in June 1944.

Convoy protection usually consisted of two MAC ships, although at times as many as four were used. Routine flying patrols were always at the side or ahead of convoys — an astern patrol could prove disastrous for a Swordfish if the wind freshened. On one occasion when this happened the ship unhappily had to watch its Swordfish gradually disappear astern until it was no longer recorded on the radar screen — never to be seen again. Each carrier did a 12-hour turn of duty but if there were

three of them one could stand down. One of the problems was whales. It was not unknown for crews to mistake the large brown shape with a vertical lump amidships for a U-boat. Sub-Lt John K. G. Taylor's logbook for 9 August 1944 reads: 'Swordfish NF199, pilot Lt Johnstone — Viper patrol — sighted and attacked dead whale.'

There are many interesting and humorous stories attached to the MAC ships but unfortunately space precludes their use here. The last known contact with a U-boat was on 20 April 1945 when a Swordfish from *Empire Mac-Andrew* dropped two depth charges on a periscope with no apparent results. The last operational squadron to fly the Swordfish, 836, was disbanded on **21 May 1945.**

WHAT WAS IT LIKE TO FLY, DAD?

Below:
The moment of truth: coming in over the round-down for the deck landing of your life — the first one!
Public Archives of Canada

Such might be the question put to any Fleet Air Arm aircrew who were fortunate enough to fly in the Swordfish. This extract from the book *Bring back my Stringbag* by Lt-Cdr John Godley (later Lord Kilbracken) is probably one of the best accounts of what it was like to fly this giant biplane.

'How to convey the experience of piloting a Stringbag, which certainly ranks among the most remarkable aircraft ever invented? A makey-learn pilot converting to any other operational type at once knew he was handling a lethal steely machine that meant business, at least if compared with training aircraft. Not so the Stringbag, bless her dear old heart. She seemed to have been left in the war by mistake, to belong to another age,

though she'd been in production for only six years. It was almost impossible to believe that it was with this, though she might be a great lark to fly, that we'd soon be expected to go tearing into action. Yet she had the most wondrous virtues. She was almost totally foolproof. You could take nearly any liberty, fly her far beyond textbook capability. The willingness and ability to do so was a major part of being a worthy Stringbag pilot and she always saw you through. She was absolutely stable and even at almost the lowest speeds the controls were firm and positive. Scream down from an immense height in a dive, the speed would stay well below 200 kt and you could haul back on the stick for all you were worth — a fast firm pull-out with no fear of that old enemy, the high speed stall. No one ever wrenched the wings off a Strinbag though on the ground they could be folded fore and aft with an amazingly simple manual mechanism to reduce the space they'd take up on a carrier.

'Cut back speed and the slots would come out on the leading edges of the mainplanes, decrease wing-loading and thereby the speed of stall, to about 65kt. Slower still and she would waffle ever so slightly but full control was maintained. When at last stalling speed was neared at 58 knots or so, even if at this moment you pulled back hard on the stick, her nose would drop sedately, very gently

earthwards and she would fall in relative equilibrium through perhaps 100ft until flying speed was regained. She'd come home though riddled with bullets like a collander.

'There was nothing to go wrong so long as the Pegasus III engine kept ticking over. My "Peggy", as it happened, was twice to let me down, but such ill-luck was exceptional. She could keep going with two cylinders shot away.

'The absurdly low handling speed of a Stringbag made it possible to operate when even the birds were walking (as

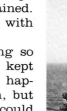

123

Right:
Formation flying was an essential part of flying training prior to joining a squadron. In this prewar shot the lads from Gosport show us how it should be done. *IWM (MH45)*

Below:
Treasured moments — off solo in the Swordfish. *British Aerospace*

Far right, top:
Time to join a front-line unit, which means landing on an operational carrier for the first time, so here goes... *IWM (A18255)*

Far right, centre:
... coming up astern, carrier into wind, approach OK... *IWM (A18257)*

Far right, bottom:
... over the round-down, watch the 'bats', keep the wings level, did I put the hook down? Don't want to make a hash of it, first time and all that...

we used to put it). The carrier could pitch all over the Arctic but, if the wind over the flight deck was 55kt, the Stringbag's forward speed relative to the deck would be a mere five knots, no more than a fast walk. Sometimes I've had to motor her in and touch down above stalling speed to keep up with the ship. Indeed, a Stringbag in my squadron was patrolling some way astern of a convoy when a gale blew up ahead; the convoy was steaming into wind at only 10kt but the pilot ran out of petrol before he could catch up and was never seen again. We were completely exposed to the elements. I need hardly mention that our cockpits were unheated, though the pilot (but not his observer or TAG in their separate cockpit behind him) derived some benefit from the "Peggy's" close proximity. This did indeed make it chilly on the Murmansk run at below zero Fahrenheit, but to feel the wind in your face is a joy seldom known to today's flyers.

'And despite everything I remember with perfect clarity that my chief impression as I first flew a Stringbag, over springtime Fifeshire fields and out across the Forth, was of her enormous size and power. I was flying this damn great thing all by myself.'

From the observer's position it was a bit different and David Corkhill recalls his impressions of those days:
'One thing I remember vividly of that period was the incredibly bitter cold of that winter. In January 1940 one aircraft reported a temperature of −18°C on the thermometer carried on one of the starboard mainplane struts. Perhaps one of every Swordfish crew's abiding memories is of the terrible penetrating cold in all three cockpits. It froze one to the marrow in bad weather and produced a hypothermic torpor which made thought and action very difficult. At this stage of the war (1940) we were not issued with clothing which was sufficient to combat these conditions. Most of us supplemented flying clothing with our own private purchases. Mine consisted of a pair of sheepskin gloves which I could slip on and off for navigating and a pair of oiled wool heavy stockings. On Russian convoys it was not unknown for pilots to have to be lifted from their cockpits at the end of a patrol. The observer and air gunner, although exposed, did have the luxury of being able to move around.

Right:
CUT . . . magic, it's a good one. *IWM (A27599+A18260)*

Below right:
The view from the deck . . . *IWM (A18269)*

Right:
. . . second wire — oh well, better than the third . . . *IWM (A18876)*

Below:
. . . now I can taxi forward and park — super, fantastic feeling, you know, landing on a carrier. *Royal Netherlands Navy*

'It is perhaps worth mentioning the long-range fuel tank which fitted in and on top of the observer's cockpit. This reduced the aircraft to a two-seater and prevented the use of the ASV. On these occasions, sitting in the air gunner's cockpit was an observer's nightmare. A tubular air intake vent was situated on the top of the tank shaped like an inverted letter "L". This had a cork stuck in the end to stop the fuel gushing out on take-off. If this happened, it invariably doused the observer's head and shoulders in petrol. The cork had to be removed when airborne to allow the fuel to flow. The cork was fastened to the vent tube by a piece of cord to prevent it blowing away. Inevitably, the cork snapping around on the end of the cord in the slipstream led to its early disappearance. It then became necessary on every take-off for the observer to be sitting on the outside edge of the cockpit so that he could put his hand over the mouth of the vent. Taking one's hand away too soon resulted in a sleeve full of petrol. As well as these indignities, the observer was required to switch off the transfer cock on the bottom of the tank when asked by the pilot. This involved getting the head and shoulders through an incredibly small space where the back of the TAG's seat had been. Meanwhile the observer's legs had been manoeuvred up on to the gun mounting. It was not unknown for a highly embarrassed observer to become stuck in this position! The further disadvantage was that the tank shape funnelled the slipstream into the TAG's cockpit, making conditions even more uncomfortable.

'Sub-Lt John Miller, who joined 819 Squadron in 1942, devised a most ingenious modification. By separating the radio transmitter and receiver in the TAG's cockpit, he managed to fit the ASV display tube between the two. This was a tremendous help to night navigation. When we reported what we had done, feeling rather pleased with ourselves, we were told to put everything back where it had been because we had not submitted details, nor asked permission, etc, etc. Needless to say, we left things exactly as they were.'

Far left:
An operational pilot at last — Sub-Lt Howell in front of his Swordfish of 833 Squadron at Jamaica in 1941 after a spell with 810 Squadron in Ark Royal.
Lt-Cdr M. B. W. Howell

Left:
Of course, every anti-submarine man has to have an observer — and who better than Lt David Corkhill DSC, RN, to show what every good naval airman should look like.
David Corkhill

Although well known, this
picture depicts Swordfish
L2742 '529' operating from
the Rock of Gibraltar.
Swordfish, shore-based or
on floats, monitored the
Straits of Gibraltar
throughout the war.